EMERALD BAY

By

Bob Bitchin

Bob Bitchin

Other books by Bob Bitchin

- *Brotherhood of Outlaws*
- *Biker*
- *Letters from the Lost Soul*

Emerald Bay

Copyright © 2002 by Robert Lipkin
All rights reserved, including the right to reproduce this book and / or portions thereof in any form whatsoever.

This book is a work of fiction. Names, Characters, places and incidents are either the product of the author's imagination, or are used fictitiously. Any resemblance to actual events, locals or persons, living or dead, is entirely coincidental.

Emerald Bay is published by FTW Publishing Inc. FTW Publishing grants discounts on the purchase of 12 or more copies of the same title. For further details, please write to:
FTW Publishing Inc.
Box 668
Redondo Beach, CA 90277

Printed and manufactured in Canada
First edition: May, 2000

Cover illustration by Bob Bitchin
Library of Congress Catalog Card Number

ISBN: 0-9662182-2-1

If you purchase this book without a cover, you should be aware that this book is stolen property. It was reported as "unsold and destroyed" to the publisher, and neither the author or publisher has received any payment for the "unstripped book"

LIVING THE DREAM

Robert "Bob Bitchin" Lipkin was born in Los Angeles, California in 1944. He spent 28 years riding motorcycles around the United States and Europe, writing of his experiences in all of the major motorcycle magazines of the 70s and 80s. In the early 70s he acted as roustabout and body guard for a famous motorcycle daredevil, and later produced "CycleExpo," a large California motorcycle show. During most of those years he lived aboard various sailboats that he would buy in rundown condition, and restore to sell. He went on to create *Biker News*, *Biker Magazine*, and *Tattoo Magazine* in the early 80s. In 1988 he sold his magazines and retired. He spent several years sailing the Pacific; first on his Formosa 51' center cockpit ketch *Lost Soul*, and then on an aft cockpit Formosa 51', *Predator*. In 1991 he purchased a derelict 68' ketch which he renamed *Lost Soul*. A year later, after extensive repairs he departed with his lady friend Jody on a voyage that would take them to the far corners of the Earth. Five years, and 50,000 miles later He returned and founded *Latitudes & Attitudes*, a sailing and cruising magazine that can be found on cruising boats around the world. Bob Bitchin lives aboard his vessel *Lost Soul* with his (now) wife, Jody, in cruising ports worldwide, and in his home port at The Portofino Marina and Yacht Club in Southern California.

Don't dream your life; live your dreams!
Bob Bitchin

Emerald Bay

Dedication

This book is dedicated to my mother, Mary Lipkin. Her confidence in me made me truly believe that I could do anything if I only dreamed it and wanted it bad enough.

Special thanks

I would like to thank the following people for their help in putting this book together. They know what they did.

Bob Sable (may he rest in peace)
Glenn Stewart (Only the best die young)
Richard Bustillo (Let's ride!)
Captain Alan Byer (You edit reel gud!)

Emerald Bay

Prologue

   A small gray fishing boat loomed out of the heavy fog that surrounded the yacht *Rogue*. The name could barely be read on the stern of the large boat through the fog. She was a William Garden designed Ketch, well over 50 feet in length with her main mast sticking over 60 feet into the air and disappearing in the fog. She had graceful lines reminiscent of the sailing ships of old with her clipper bow and canoe stern. Heavy black accent and boot stripes set off the stark white of her hull, with black sail covers keeping in touch with her pirate ancestry. Her raised poop deck was highly varnished, and she was a stately vessel, as she sat calmly in her mooring. A small anchor light was visible at the top of her mast and she was alone in the bay, looking as is she had sailed in from out of the past.
   Jake Simms took the wheel of a small fishing boat and swung it starboard, pulling near the boarding ladder of the *Rogue*. Jake made fast to the side with a bow and stern line, throwing a looped end over the bow and midships cleat on the large boat and tying the dead ends to the cleats on his *Sea Ox*.

Robert "Rabbit" Moriega was the other occupant of the small boat. He was dressed in a wetsuit. It was all black and had a small yellow patch with a black hand over the heart that read "Body Glove". On his back was an aluminum 80 scuba tank painted flat black. He put his regulator in his mouth, checked his weight belt and timer, then dove into the dark clear waters of Emerald Bay, clutching a small bundle.

Jake lit a cigarette and watched the bubbles move around the stern of the boat. They showed the path taken by his partner. Rabbit took his time locating just the right place for his parcel. Even though it was dark and foggy, the water was so clear he could see his partner disappear under the keel of the yacht. Jake was nervous and kept his eyes in constant motion around the small, curved bay.

It was about 5 A.M., and the sun hadn't cleared the horizon yet. Even if it did, the fog would keep it dark enough so as to cover their presence.

The bay was completely void of other craft. The white mooring buoys bobbed in the calm harbor and even the surf noise was subdued by the heavy air. It was off season for Catalina, and the cool damp air was keeping the hundreds of boaters that usually visited Emerald Bay snug in their harbors in Marina Del Rey, King Harbor, and Long Beach. California boaters were a spoiled lot, and the least little bit of weather would keep them tied to the docks.

The sound of a rock rolling down the hillside of the bay brought Jake back to reality, and he swung his nightvision monocular up and swept the road that ran around the small cove. Even though it was off season, there were still a few people that lived on the west end of Catalina, and he couldn't afford to be spotted here.

The few minutes seemed like an eternity, as he checked every bush on the hillside, and only after he saw the mountain goats almost at the top of the

Emerald Bay

hillside, did he relax. He remembered that there were stories of buffalo and mountain goats on the island, and even some wild pigs. He was just feeling a little jumpy. They couldn't afford to be seen here, nor could they leave any evidence of their visit.

Edging the clear dark waters was a sheer cliff, almost 200 feet high, that went from end to end of the cove in a sweeping curve. At the top of the cliff was a gravel access road that went from the landing at Twin Harbors to the small camp, a half mile to the west of the cove. At the base of the cliff was a white sandy beach, with sand so white it seemed to glow even in the fog and darkness. At one end sat two tall palm trees, remnants of a movie that was filmed back in Hollywood's heyday, The original *Mutiny on the Bounty*, with Clark Gable.

Sitting a couple of hundred feet off the base of the cliff, across the clear emerald waters that gave the bay its name, was the reef, fronted by Indian Rock. When the rock was viewed form certain angles it took the shape of an Indian head searching the sky.

The reef was what made Emerald Bay the tourist Mecca that it was for boaters. The only way to get to Emerald Bay was by boat or by a small and very dangerous dirt road from Isthmus Cove. Sitting about 100 feet offshore, was the reef, protecting the small beach and keeping the sand clean and white. It had evolved over thousands of years and its stories were many.

When his partner surfaced, Jake helped him into the boat. It was built for diving and used a lot by the Coast Guard. Though it was only 20 feet long, it was solid and obviously she was made for strength.

"Everything Ok?" Jake asked as Rabbit climbed up the boarding ladder.

"Yeah, no problems."

Jake started the engine, and they headed slowly out

3

of the Bay. The darkness was lifting, but the fog hid the island before they even cleared the reef. The muffled sound of the 200 horsepower Honda four-stroke outboard, was lost in the fog, and they watched the compass intently. Once clear of the island, they came to a 30° heading and the throttle was pushed to full, as they skimmed over the calm waters of the San Pedro channel at over 25 miles an hour. The 25 miles back across the San Pedro channel went fast.

It was almost 7 AM as they were cruising past the stately *Queen Mary* and the Spruce Goose. They turned into a small bay right in front of the Queen and tied up at a mooring in the Queensway Marina. It was the same buoy they had left from just three hours earlier, and they knew as soon as they were gone, the company would have the boat picked up and moved back to the government docks.

They stashed the keys to the boat in the small compartment near the battery as they had been instructed to do and headed back to the land.

The boat had done its job well. The orange and white Coast Guard colors had been covered with a gray substance that looked like wallpaper. From a distance, the boat looked like any of a hundred rental boats out for some fishing off Palos Verdes or in the Catalina Channel. Jake knew it wouldn't take fifteen or twenty minutes for the paper to be peeled off and the boat would be back on duty by the 9 am shift.

The fog was starting to lift and it was a normal May morning for the coast of Southern California. Low clouds and fog in the early morning turning to a warm sunny day as the sun warmed the air and burned off the moisture.

Fishing boats started to fill the harbor as Jake wheeled the plain white Dodge out of the lot and onto the on-ramp of the Harbor freeway.

He turned to Rabbit.
"Well what do you think? Did that little swim warm you up for some breakfast?"

Bob Bitchin

1

Treb Lincoln rolled over slowly. His eyes were still closed, but he could smell the faint perfume Karen had worn the night before. He rested his arm over her body and snuggled closer. Her long blonde hair fell across his face and he inhaled deeply, loving even the smell of her.

He thought back to the night of lovemaking and smiled to himself. Even after two years it was better each time they were together. At 22 years old, she knew a lot about life and a lot more about pleasing him. He unconsciously slid his hand down her hard stomach and caressed her womanhood. He could hear her starting to breathe heavier and he knew she was awake. He just lay there enjoying the feeling. An infinitesimal smile came to her face, and Treb took a deep breath to fill the feeling he always got inside when he looked at her.

When they'd met two years ago, she had just turned 19, but had the street smarts of a much older woman. She'd been on her own for a couple of years and she was working in a massage parlor owned by one of the bike clubs Treb was visiting up in Utah. She had a strong effect on him from the first night they met, and a few weeks later, as he was riding across the country, he called her and had her fly out to join him. Ever since they had been a team, and they were both happier than they had ever been in their lives.

Once again the feelings she brought out in him started to flood through him, and he reached out to her as she rolled over on top of him.

She grabbed his wrists and tried to pin him to the bed as if she were going to rape him.

"You can't rape the willing," he laughed, and rolled her over onto her back.

Just as he rolled on top of her and started to pin her hands over her head in the playful game they always enjoyed, the phone rang. He thought about ignoring it, but before he could make the final decision, Karen rolled playfully to one side, unceremoniously dumping him off the bed, stark naked.

Then she rolled across the king sized bed and grabbed the phone. He was helpless because he was laughing so hard. When she rolled over to get the phone, the electric blanket pulled the cord, which wrapped around the leg of the nightstand, pulling it over and knocking the TV off the nightstand next to it. The sound of the TV hitting the ground, had scared their tomcat *Fishbait* out of a sound dream, and he had cleared the pillows on the bed, landing square on Karen's bare ass, with all claws at full attention.

Treb was still roaring as he took the phone she had dropped.

He said hello and was still laughing as he watched Karen blotting small droplets of blood off of her derriere. Fishbait looked extremely annoyed at the indignities he'd had to endure, and he hiked his tail showing Karen his asshole as if to say, "check this out!" Then he stalked off the bed and into the kitchen.

Treb heard Rom's voice come through the phone. He and Rom had been friends for almost twenty years, ever since the old days when they were riding Harley's and raising hell. They'd been through a lot together over the years and were as close as two people could be.

"Hey man, what's going on there? Sounds like Robin Williams' giving a free concert over there. What's so funny?"

Treb considered the chain of events that led up to the phone being answered and decided against trying to explain.

Instead he said "Never mind, you wouldn't understand. What's up?"

He stood there listening and watched Karen as she got out of bed, moving slow and sexy to try and get him aroused as she walked into the bathroom. He heard the shower start to run, and realized that Rom was still talking.

".. so I thought maybe you and Karen would want to come by for breakfast on the way to the church. The wedding isn't until noon and it's only nine o'clock now. Whadaya think?"

Treb could picture Rom, probably up to his knees in beer cans and wine bottles from the party last night and probably still wearing his old favorite flannel shirt.

Ol' Rom was more excited about Treb getting married than Treb was. The fact that he was best man made him feel pretty good and almost made up for the jealousy he had felt about Karen taking his friend away.

Treb thought a minute about it and decided he would rather go jump in the shower with Karen then fight roaches away from warm beer and cold pizza at Rom's house.

He spoke into the phone, "No thanks Rom, I got something to do here. Why don't you get Dick and go out to breakfast. And I'll meet you at the church at eleven?"

Dick Bondano was the third member of the Three Musketeers, and for years they had been inseparable. Treb almost felt like a traitor getting married, but after 40 years he had finally found what he wanted, and didn't want to let her escape.

"Ok, Treb, but don't forget the little party afterwards. You've been sniveling out for too long, so me and Dick have decided it's time you party with us."

"Yeah," he smiled, "well I can still party your little ass under the table!" Treb laughed.

There weren't many people that could call Rom's ass little, but Treb was one of them. Even though Rom was near 200 pounds and six feet tall, Treb's 295 and 6'4" frame made most people small in comparison.

"We'll see this afternoon." Rom hesitated. "Are you sure you're doing the right thing?"

Treb thought about how sure he really was and smiled.

"Yeah bro, I'm sure. See you in awhile."

After he hung up the phone, he walked into the bathroom where he heard the water running in the shower. He could make out the full figure of the girl he loved, through the thin, almost transparent shower curtain. Karen as a little over five feet tall, but she was built like a proverbial brick shithouse. Her dark blue eyes were probably her strongest and most striking feature, but at the moment, eyes were the last thing

10

Treb was thinking about.
 He looked into the large mirror behind the sink and rubbed his beard. He had sported a beard for 18 years, but had almost decided to cut it off for the wedding. Karen talked him into keeping it. He stepped back and looked into the mirror.
 Staring back at him was a bush of dark blonde hair with two blue eyes stuck just below. He wasn't handsome, but he wouldn't scare many people either. He had a heavy, dark blonde beard and mustache covering most of his face, and there were a few scars from bygone younger days. He stood transfixed as he recalled where most of them came from. Some folks said it gave him character and most of his friends figured that's what he was. A character. Though he had been lifting weights off and on for 15 years, he was still no Arnold Schwartzenegger. All things considered, he didn't look too bad for 40 years of hard life. He owned his own gym now and found he was working out more, but he still had a long way to go. He flexed and looked at himself in the mirror and laughed.
 "What are you laughing at?" he heard Karen say from the shower.
 "Oh," he started, " I was just thinking what all the other girls are going to do to you when they find out you got me."
 With that, he saw the shower door open and Karen came out with a soaking wet towel. He watched her naked body sway as she came at him. The muscles in her long legs flexing with each step. She wrapped the wet towel around his neck with a flick of her arm, laughing as she did it. Then she pulled him to her and wrapped her arms around him. She hooked one leg behind him and wrapped his body with hers. He ran his hand down her wet back and rested his hand on her firm behind. Soon they were laying on the floor of the

bathroom with the shower door open and the water coming out soaking the carpet. Fishbait walked through the door and looked at them like they were crazy, then curled up on the damp towel and watched, licking his paws.
 .. But they didn't notice. They were both too engrossed with their lovemaking to see it, or for that matter to care. Even the pounding on the floor from the apartment below, 20 minutes later, didn't disturb them, as they fell deep into the trance they both loved so much.

2

Al Huntington sat back in the deep leather seats of his black Mercedes 600S and looked thought the darkly tinted windows, lost in thought. "If I can pull this deal off, I'll have more money than I could ever need." he thought. Actually he already had more then he could ever spend, but he just couldn't escape the poverty of his youth.

Sitting next to him was Eva Ortiz. She was 19 years old and beautiful. That was the only word to describe her. Her hair was black as coal, and her blue/green eyes showed that there was some Anglo in her family's past. The combination was striking, and her soft, dark complexion only set it off more.

She was wearing a simple black skirt with a white

peasant blouse. Of course it had cost Al over $800 on Rodeo Drive for the outfit, but Huntington only wanted the best to surround him. He only owned the best, and he owned her. Therefore she had to be the best.

He felt he deserved the best. He had worked his way to where he was by fighting all the way. His early days in East Los Angeles, when he was known as Alberto Herrera, were a constant fight.

He learned early no one would give you anything without getting something in return. He learned the hard way when his mother died. He was only thirteen then, but the picture of what happened was still vivid in his mind.

He cut school that day. When you're 13 years old and living in southern California, sometimes it was just too nice to be in school. Al and some of his Homies were sitting behind their favorite 7-11 just killing time and waiting. All the while they kept a close eye on the clerk behind the counter. The guard, they knew, stayed in the back office with a shotgun. They had plenty of time but they also had the impatience of youth. Soon the office door inside the store opened and the guard stepped out. He looked around and walked into the bathroom, signaling the clerk.

Suddenly the boys were in action.

Three of the youths walked around to the front of the store and went through the front door. They were particularly loud and obnoxious. In a couple of minutes the clerk was trying to clear them out of the store. He kept glancing at the restroom door.

Meanwhile Al and his friend Freddie picked up two cases of Budweiser and headed for home. The others would leave the store in a minute and pick up whatever they could grab on the way out.

They made their way through the alleys and back

street heading to Angelo's. Angelo was the neighborhood dealer. He had style.

Al thought back on what he used to consider style. Angelo had a five year old Cadillac, lived in a three bedroom house on 123rd St, and had two old ladies living with him.

Yeah, back then, that was style.

At least once a week Al would find a way to get something to trade to Angelo for drugs. It didn't matter how little, he could make money once he had his hands on some drugs. Marijuana, cocaine, heroin, or speed would quickly turn into hard cash. By the time Al was 13, he had a steady clientele and was moving at least an ounce a week to the kids at school. He spent every dime on giving himself style. By the time he was 15 he was driving a new Lincoln. It was lowered and painted Candy Apple Red. The paint job alone cost him over $2,000, but he didn't care. It was style.

He never touched drugs himself. His mother wouldn't like it and he loved his mother more than anything on the earth. His world revolved around her.

When she died, she was just 33 years old and she died of poverty. She was worn out and just tired of living. No matter how hard she worked at the office building downtown, she never seemed to get ahead. Even the money he gave her didn't seem to make a difference. One day he came home and she was in the hospital. They called it Cancer. He knew better. She died of poverty.

And he swore that was one disease he would never catch.

He stayed in school, not to learn, but to keep his connections. By the time he was out he'd made a small fortune. Now Angelo was buying from him, and he controlled the drugs for his whole barrio.

After years of building his business he finally decided

15

he had made enough to get out of the area and move up.

To a young man from East Los Angeles, that meant a move up into the hills of La Puente. He found a vacant lot looking over his "city" and built a 3,000 square foot house, with an 8 foot wall around it and broken glass embedded in the concrete top. He had a pool table in the game room and a wet bar by the patio. He had it made.

His candy red Lincoln was soon replaced by the status car of the 90's, a black Mercedes 600S. The windows were tinted dark and the seats were covered with black sheepskins. It had been slightly lowered and sported Centra rims and Continental Tires. The same tires he'd seen on a Rolls' once. A small antenna on the back window told of the cellular phone inside, and he felt he's finally made it to the top.

And then he met Armando.

All of a sudden his idea of making it was boosted to a higher level. Armando was the man he bought his coke from, and he lived in Beverly Hills.

Al's low Mercedes pulled into the driveway of a Tudor styled mansion, bringing him back to the present. He gazed around the open expanse of yard and saw surveillance cameras spotted all around the perimeter. His two bodyguards climbed out of the front seat of the car and looked around. When they were sure it was all clear they opened the back door for him to get out.

Al stepped out and held his hand out for Eva. She looked at him for a second and then took his hand, gracefully sliding across the seat to get out. The two guards separated. One in front and one behind as they walked up the stairs to the entrance of the mansion. Another camera watched as they approached.

Al looked at the house. Someday, he thought, someday I too will live like this.

The door was opened by a man that looked like a football player. He was wearing a pair of light gray slacks and a black T-shirt. Over the shirt he wore an expensive light blue sports jacket that didn't quite hide the .45 automatic in his shoulder holster. He was very polite and asked them into the entryway. The bodyguards were told to wait outside. Once the door closed behind him he could see two more guards. One on the balcony overlooking the entrance, and another a little way down the hall.

"I'm sorry", said the football player," but it's my job."

And with that he patted Al down. Then he searched Eva's purse and hesitated for a minute.

"I understand," said Al.

The football player then patted Eva down.

Actually Al couldn't care less if the guy got a feel. She was just his property. Window dressing.

When the search was over and the guard was sure they had no weapons, he led them down a large hallway filled with classic paintings in large gold frames. Then the football player knocked lightly on a large pair of double doors that stood almost ten feet high.

Someday! Al thought. Someday!

The door opened and they were escorted into a large elegant room. At the far end was a picture window that overlooked most of Los Angeles. The home had one of the best views in Truesdale Estates. You could see from Long Beach all across to Point Dume. In the distance was Catalina Island, shrouded in haze.

There were three very large overstuffed sofas arranged in a "U" shape in front of the window. A large white marble fireplace sat to one side, and even though it was a warm day outside, there was a fire going. There were three men seated around the white marble coffee table, and a large man was pouring drinks at the matching marble bar. Al recognized him

17

as another guard.

Al didn't recognize the other two men. When he reached the seating area, Armando smiled.

"Al, this is Jose Tirantia. They call him *El Tigre*. I've been telling him about you and he asked to meet you."

The man stood up, and for the first time in his 35 years, Al felt a cold shock of fear deep in his stomach. The man was about 5'9" and a little on the heavy side, but what got to Al was his eyes. They were as cold as ice and looked right through him. This was a man to be feared. He could feel it deep inside.

"It's good to meet you," said Al. "How can I be of service?"

"Mucho gusto, Alberto. Por favor, forgive my English, as it is not so good. I am just in the country for a little while, on business and Armando tells me you can be.. Como se dice?.. Ah yes, trusted. He says you can be trusted. Is this so?"

"Of course. If you are a friend of Armando you can ask anything of me. Any friend of his is a friend of mine."

"Gracias, gracias. Es la senorita su esposa?.. Your wife? Es muy bonita." And with that the man held out his hand to Eva.

Eva smiled at him with a melting smile.

"Thank you, senor." She smiled at him again. "My name is Eva. Mucho gusto."

Tirantia stood up and stared at the girl for a very long time. Then as if he realized where he was, he spoke to her.

"Ah, you speak my language well. You are from the south, si?" It was obvious the man was shocked by her looks, more so than most men. He saw something in her that he couldn't quite put together.

"Si, mi familia es en Guatemala," she said.

The man looked as if he were in deep thought.

"Guatemala? What region? What city?" His questions were almost an inquisition.

She was a little frightened by his stare, but more so by Al's.

She knew she had better leave the conversation. The look on Al's face told her in no uncertain terms.

"Chichetenango", she replied, "in the South."

Tirantia seemed to file the information away in his head, and then turned back and smiled at Al.

Since the third man was not introduced, Al assumed he was another guard.

They sat for a minute looking at the view, and after the drinks were served, Armando made a small signal with his hand. The two guards started to leave the room.

Al turned to Eva.

"My dear, I think you should powder your nose." He looked at his host, "Perhaps one of these men would show her the house?"

Once again Armando signaled and one of the men held the door open for her.

When they were alone, business could be discussed. The meeting lasted less than an hour.

. . . .

Al was in a daze as he walked form the mansion after the meeting. He hardly noticed the looks between his new "friend" Tirantia and Eva. All he could think about was seeing all his dreams were about to come true. If things went as planned, in a matter of months he would be worth millions. "If only my mother could see me now," he thought. He got into the car, settled back into the deep, soft leather, and considered the meeting.

It seems that Jose Tirantia, known in his home country of Costa Rica as "EL Tigre, was not just another drug dealer. He was the source of supply for his supplier. Now, for some reason, and he didn't really care what it was, they wanted him to start handling all of Armando's business. Not only that, but they wanted to increase the volume.

The black car pulled out of the driveway and headed back to his home in La Puente. Al sat back and was lost in thought.

No longer was he thinking in pounds. No more selling ounces to hyped up druggies. Soon he would be moving hundreds of pounds. Tons, if they were accurate in their estimates. He'd be doing millions of dollars a week.

The first step was the meeting. They had someone they wanted him to meet with and it had to be in a very safe place. What confused him was why it had to be in the united States. It was obvious that the man was in Costa Rica and it would be easy for Al to just fly there. When he suggested they do it that way, they looked at each other for a minute and then said it would have to be in a place where not only wouldn't the man be seen, but he couldn't be seen with El Tigre either.

It took almost an hour for them to agree on a safe meeting spot. It was only after Armando suggested meeting on a boat, things fell into place. Since he had been successful bringing in his biggest shipments through Catalina Island, it was a natural and seemed the best and safest place for a meet.

For years the smugglers had used the vacation island of Catalina as a clean way of bringing their drugs into the country. They would load a sailboat with the contraband in Costa Rica and then sail it out a thousand miles to sea. They would then turn north and come straight in to Catalina. When they would be approached by the Coast Guard, as they were three out of four times, they would simply cut the cargo off the stern, where it was tied on in 55 gallon drums. They would then mark the latitude and longitude in code on a piece of paper as they watched the weighted barrels sink to the bottom.

After the routine boarding, in which nothing was ever found, they would sail slowly towards the island. They would anchor for a day or two, and then return to the spot and retrieve the barrels.

On each 55 gallon drum, was a radio activated flotation device. They would simply hit a switch and the drum would float to the surface. They would then tie the drums off the stern, recharge the floatation device in the event they were boarded again, and pull into Emerald Bay.

Then they would have two or three small sailboats sail over on the busy weekends and they would transfer 100 pound lots to each boat. They had never been caught.

Al was told to wait for a call. They would tell him where and when the meet was set for. He was nervous as a cat.

Bob Bitchin

3

Eva was calm and serene as they left Armando's. Even though she had just met Tirantia, she thought maybe she had found a way out of the cage that Al "Huntington" Herrera had built her into over the last four years. She could see how he feared the new man. There was something about him that scared her, but it scared Al too, and that made her feel good. The whole time the man was asking her questions, it seemed more than just polite conversation. He'd asked her about her family, where she was from, and when she was born. Somehow she knew he would change her life.

When she was 15 years old, she and her mother had come to America to find their dream. She never knew her father. He was a young man from her mother's village, that was taken to fight as a soldier and was never heard from again. It was he who had passed on the blue/green eyes that made her stand out. If their ancestry could have been traced, they would have known their ancestors went back to the great Spanish legend, Hernando Cortez, and the blue/green eyes were their only legacy.

Their village was very poor, but no worse than a thousand other villages in war torn Guatemala. They probably would have stayed there, but for Eva's mother. She wanted more for Eva then what she'd had. Since Eva's father had been taken before they could be married, she was looked down on in the very religious village. She was an outcast.

A girlfriend of her mother had gone to America to meet her husband. This was when Eva was just three or four years old. Almost five years went by before Eva's mother heard from this friend, and when she did, she started saving for the trip north.

Her friend told of unbelievable riches. Her husband was a dishwasher in a small restaurant, but he had his own car. In the village no one had a car. They also had something called a television, like a radio but with pictures. In the village there was only one radio, and it was at the small tienda, or store.

And the woman didn't even make her own clothes. Her husband made so much money they bought their clothes at a store.

She knew she had to get there, for herself and for her daughter.

It took another five years for her to get enough money for them to leave.

The first part of the adventure was easy. They simply crossed the border into Mexico where the jungle was thickest. No border guards. No problems. Then they got on a bus, and in two days they arrived

Emerald Bay

in Tijuana.

Eva had been raised in a small town and the sights around Tijuana kept her enthralled. All of the pretty clothes that you could just go into a shop and buy. The cars, the boys, there were so many of them, and they all stared at her when she walked by. She didn't know why.

But the reason was obvious to her mother. Eva, at 15 years of age, was a woman, and a beautiful woman at that. Her mother had done her best to keep her clothed in oversized dresses that would hide her womanly curves, but now that was becoming almost impossible.

Aside from her well developed body, her beauty couldn't be hidden by anything. She had grown into a striking woman, and no clothing or dirty hair could hide it. Her thick black hair and strong blue/green eyes shone through any covering.

And this would be both their downfall and salvation.

Tijuana is not known as a friendly town, and it is the most vicious to those who don't understand the depths of degradation that civilized man can drop to.

One day Eva and her mother heard of a man that could get them across the border, and they went to see him. As soon as he saw Eva, his lust could not be controlled. He had to have her.

All of the other coyotes were charging $200 for each person crossing. To assure they went with him he told them it would be just half that. Just $100 apiece. They were excited, and spent the next two days getting ready for the big day. They went shopping for the first new store-bought clothes that Eva would ever wear.

First they bought her undergarments. Panties and a bra. She had never worn a bra and didn't know how to wear it. Once she had the underclothes, they bought her a brightly colored, full skirt and a plain white blouse. The last item they bought was a bright red cloth belt that she wrapped around her waist twice and tied. When she was dressed, her mother looked at her, full of pride. She was more beautiful than even her mother could believe.

But while they were buying clothes and getting ready, their coyote was getting ready too.

He knew a man in Los Angeles whom he dealt with, that would pay a lot of money for a girl as pretty as Eva. He had dealt with him many times, bringing him marijuana, and he knew he had the money to pay. There were just two problems, both of which he knew he could overcome.

One was the mother. No one wants to buy a woman with an old hag along as a companion.

And the other was his own lust. He could get more for her if she was a virgin, but his loins weren't deterred by the thought of money.

The day finally came and the two women met with the twenty other people who were going across. Early in the afternoon they were all given small packages to carry and then loaded into a sewage truck. A false bottom was set in, and when it was snug in place, sewage was dumped on top. The false bottom didn't fit very well, and soon the heat and smell inside was almost unbearable.

They sat in the truck for three hours as it worked its way through the back streets and alleys of Tijuana and into the line of trucks going across the border. Their coyote was good at his profession, and soon the truck was wheeling north into the promised land.

It had just turned dark when the truck pulled off the road and into a warehouse. The coyote had his men open the truck and unload everyone. He lined them up and took the packages from them. Each package contained a kilo of marijuana that he was bringing in for his friend and new benefactor, Al Huntington.

He split the people into two groups. Eva and her

mother were ushered into a small office in the rear of the warehouse. The rest were herded out back.

Eva was so relieved to be across the border that she didn't even think about what was going on. However, her mother had seen the look in the eyes of the coyote, and she didn't like it. She was getting worried.

Once they were in the office, the coyote sat on the edge of the desk and looked at the two of them.

"The pay was not enough for you two," he said with an evil smile on his grubby face. "I tink we need a leetle more."

Eva heard two men enter the room behind her and she started getting scared. She looked at her mother, but her mother was even more afraid. She knew what was coming.

Before the mother could do anything, she was grabbed from behind by the two men. One tied a dirty handkerchief around her mouth, and the other started to tie her up.

Eva stood as if she were seeing a nightmare. She couldn't believe what was happening.

Then the coyote leered at her.

"Ok my leetle one, now eet is time to pay for your trip."

She didn't know what to do. Her mother was staring at her with wide eyes.

"Now, puta.!" He yelled at her, and tears started to roll down her cheeks.

"Wha-what do yo-you want from me?" She was almost frozen with fear. "I don't know what it is you want," she pleaded.

He walked over to her. He was large, fat, and dirty. His grubby clothes smelled putrid, and his face was covered with grime and three days of growth. When he was in front of her, he screamed at her.

"Take off your clothes, now!"

All she could do was stare at him and stutter.

"What-t-t.. what-t do-o yo-you..."

She was cut off by the back of his hand hitting her hard in the face.

"Now!"

Slowly she started to untie the red cloth belt around her waist. Tears streamed down her face. When he started to raise his hand again she just looked at him. He turned slowly to her mother.

"Your leetle girl was not well trained, is it so?" he leered at her. "Let us train her now, you and I."

And with that he hit her mother hard across the face. Blood started to flow from her nose.

Eva was in a trance now, almost in shock. She continued to take off her clothes, her eyes never leaving the face of the coyote. She could see the sweat beading on his forehead as she dropped her skirt. His eyes were wide with anticipation as her blouse came up, and she was standing there in her new panties and bra. She wasn't afraid. She was in a trance and didn't even know what she was doing.

He reached out and snatched the new bra from her, throwing it across the room. Her young breasts stood proud and free, her nipples erect from fear. She hooked her thumbs in the elastic of her panties and heard one of the men behind her breathing hard as she pulled them down over her hip. She moved in a dream, and this is what saved her sanity.

It was a dream as the dirty man pulled his penis out of his pants and grabbed her by the hair. He pulled her close and threw her to her knees. Then he shoved his filthy penis into her mouth. The smell was part of the nightmare. The mans penis kept getting larger until she thought she would choke, as he tried to ram it down her throat. It was as if she was watching unattached when he lifted her onto the dirty desk and stuck his filthy fingers into her virgin womanhood until the pain almost brought her out of it. Even when he entered her, rough and hard, she was like a person apart. Unfeeling and not responsible. While it was happening she felt no pain or shame. She almost felt proud to stand as a martyr. She had been taught all about martyrs in church.

He lifted her legs into the air and pinned her back onto the desk. Sweat was dripping on her and his breath was hot against her breast. She didn't know if it lasted a minute or twenty minutes. When he was through with her he wiped his penis on her new skirt and threw it on the floor. Eva saw blood where he wiped it and wondered where it had come from.

"Kill the woman," he said to the two men, "and then get the girl dressed and deliver her to Huntington."

With that he walked out the door of the office and out to the truck.

She looked at her mother. She couldn't think, but she knew she had to. She must not let them kill her mother.

One of them pulled a long knife out of a sheath strapped to his leg as they heard the truck start. The Coyote was leaving.

Eva thought fast. If that pig would go through all of this for her body, what about the two who were still there?

She looked into the eyes of the smallest one. She had been raised where macho was a code that people lived by, and the smaller the man, the more macho he tried to be.

"Por favor, Senor. No muerte, por favor." She looked at him, asking for her mother's life. The two men looked at her, and then at each other. They left her mother tied up on the dirty floor and walked over to Eva. For the next hour, Eva was violated again and again.

But when it was almost over, she saw her mother had untied herself and had made her way out of the room.

One of the guards was holding her hands pinned to the ground over her head as the other was deep inside of here grunting and sweating. She prayed it would end soon.

Then the first guards head dropped from his shoulders as a long machete came from nowhere. The head made a "thud" like a ripe melon as it hit the floor next to Eva. The dream/nightmare continued as the other man looked up and saw too late he was about to lose his also. He held his hand up to stop the blade, but all that did was postpone the inevitable. The machete went deep into his arm, cutting into the bone. He stared at it for a minute as blood squirted from it and his eyes were still wide as the blood covered machete came down the second time, almost severing his head form his shoulders.

Her mother stood as if she was butchering a cow. She kept swinging the sharp blade, just staring as if in a trance. After a moment she stopped and looked at Eva. Not a word was spoken.

Her mother dressed her and led her from the office, out through the warehouse. When they were outside the night air started to bring Eva back to reality. They walked around the side of the warehouse and Eva tripped on something. Her mother helped her up. They both looked to see what had tripped her.

There, in the light of the moon, were the other passengers. All of them were dead. Some had their throats cut, and others were mutilated beyond recognition.

They heard voices coming from the front of the building and started to run. From out of the night a pair of arms grabbed Eva and threw her to the ground.

"I have the girl," the voice yelled.

"I can't see the old woman," said the other voice.

"So what, the money is for this one. Let the old hag go."

That had been four years ago.

They then took her to the man she was sold to, Al Huntington.

She didn't like Al, but she had made a deal with him as soon as she was alone with him. She would not only live with him, but she would do whatever he asked of her.

And for this he would kill the coyote. Very, very slowly.

She came out of her reverie. The car was pulling into the driveway of the house, and she felt like she needed a bath.

Bob Bitchin

4

The wedding ceremony had seemed almost unreal and Treb was still in a daze as he felt the limo turn onto the Harbor freeway. He sank back into the deep leather seats and looked at the car on the freeway next to them and saw the look of confusion on the occupant's face. He figured they had probably never seen a stretch limo being followed by a hundred Harley's pull onto this piece of road before.

He smiled to himself. After over twenty years of being a biker, he still got a kick out of the way his lifestyle affected others. Was it fear? Envy? Revulsion? A combination of the three? He didn't know. All he knew was the brotherhood involved in the biker community was something that could never be replaced, and even though he had retired from the Warriors, the club was still the source of a lot of pride.

He watched as one of the older members pulled up next to the limo. It was Matt. Treb rolled down the window and reached his hand out with a bottle of champagne in it. Matt pulled alongside and grabbed it.

"Thanks, Bro," he said, as he hefted the bottle to his lips and took a healthy swig.

Treb watched as Matt dropped back into the pack and started passing the bottle. It wouldn't last long with that crowd.

It had been almost ten years ago when Matt saved Treb's life, and as he settled back into the limo, his thoughts wandered back to a rainy day just outside of Shasta in Northern California.

They'd been invited up to party with their Grant's Pass, Oregon, Chapter, and a park about ten miles from Mt. Shasta was the meeting place. They'd been up and partying for almost three days. Back then they used to mix Crystal Methamphetamine, which was "speed," in equal quantities with cocaine and Angel Dust, or PCP.. The resulting powder, when snorted, made for some very intense times.

Some citizen from town had come out to join the fun after a night at the local pub, and it was about dawn when he walked over to Cowboy and Treb standing by the fire. Cowboy was from the Nevada chapter of the club. It was drizzling lightly and they were both standing, warming their hands on the bodies of a couple young girls that had come up with the Oregon Chapter.

The dude took a fat joint out of his pocket and handed it to Cowboy. Not being one to pass on a freebee, Cowboy took out his club Zippo, with the club colors emblazoned on the side, and lit it, drawing a long, deep puff of the pungent smoke into his lungs. Then he passed it to Treb.

Treb had just taken an equally deep hit off the smoldering joint and handed it to Debbie, the girl by his side, when he started to feel "weird".

In a matter of seconds, he found himself reeling and turned to Cowboy who was staring at him in a strange kind of trance. He tried to life his arms to steady himself against Cowboy and felt as if he was wearing a lead suit. His arms weighed a couple hundred pounds. He watched Cowboy sink slowly to the ground and felt as if he was just a small person watching through his own eyes. In a second more, he was sinking to the ground too, unconscious.

His next conscious thoughts were when he came to in a van owned by one of the biker magazines that was there to do a story on the party. Matt was slapping him around pretty hard and his chest hurt. As soon as he had his eyes open, Matt was under one arm and Matt's old lady Debbie was under another, as they walked Treb around the camp for almost an hour, until he came out of it.

He later found out that his heart had stopped when a massive dose of PCP had entered his lungs. PCP is an animal tranquilizer a lot of people get high on, but usually in small doses. It seemed the guy that had joined the party, wanted to impress the bikers, so he packed over a gram into the joint he was passing. With a little PCP in it, they'd call it "Killer Weed" or "KW", but with that much in it "Killer Weed" was more than just a name.

Matt had beat pretty hard on Treb's chest to get his heart going again. The PCP had done its job and Treb was actually dead for a few seconds. Matt had been a medic in Vietnam and knew enough to administer a little "medicinal" cocaine to counteract the depressant. Cowboy had come out of the daze unharmed, as had one of the girls, but the first girl that took a hit wasn't so lucky. Her heart had stopped and they couldn't get it going again. She had died.

When the group around the fire had started hitting the ground, the guy who'd passed the KW disappeared fast. It took the club almost an hour to find him. Treb never did know exactly what had happened to him and didn't really care. Justice works itself out in the end.

That little incident had changed Treb's outlook on life. Before that time he would do any drug invented or found. It never mattered to him, but after that day he stopped doing anything but some occasional pot and maybe some alcohol. If he couldn't handle chemicals, he didn't need to take them.

He came out of his reverie and found himself staring at Karen in the back of the limo. Her face was split in half by the biggest smile he had ever seen and she was busy pulling off three or four of the bulky slips she had on under the wedding gown. As she pulled each one off she would jam it up through the sun roof and the bikes in back would go nuts trying to avoid being hit by them. Rom managed to catch one on the fly as it went past, and then looked real confused as he tried to figure out what to do with it. His dilemma was solved when a carload of college students went by laughing. He pulled up next to them and jammed it into their window.

Treb had wanted to ride his bike after the wedding, but Franko, one of the members of his old club, had gotten him the limo and he didn't want to offend him. Franko owned the limo company. Actually Treb kind of liked the luxury of it all. He reached forward to the bar and poured a glass of Scotch for himself and some white wine for Karen.

Up ahead he saw the offramp. "Catalina Cruises" it read, and the limo pulled off the freeway and headed into the parking lot.

As a wedding present Dick and Rom had bought Treb a couple of tickets to Catalina and paid for a week at the Catalina Hotel, right up the road from the casino. They had wanted to send him to Hawaii, but they didn't have the money. Besides that, the way he'd been in a dream world the past few months, he wouldn't know if he was in Katmandu or Pittsburgh.

The morning fog had burned off hours ago, and it looked like they would have perfect weather for the trip over. They could see the large red and white ship, waiting restlessly at her pier with *CATALINA EXPRESS* in large red letters on her side.

The limo dropped the two of them off at the ramp while the hundred or so bikes pulled into the parking lot. Since they didn't have a reception after the wedding it seemed only logical to have one on the way to Catalina, so all the guests had gotten tickets and they would have the whole ship to themselves on the way over to the island. There were one or two "citizens" that had planned to take the 2 o'clock express, but when they saw the pack of bikers enter the lot, they decided to wait for the next boat.

By the time they were out of the limo, Treb had already traded his only suit for something a little more comfortable. He emerged wearing his Levi's and an old black T-shirt. It had "Fuck the World" emblazoned across the chest in large white letters and the Harley logo with wings on the back.

He handed the driver a twenty as a tip and told him he would pick up his clothes at the limo office when they came back in a week or so.

"No problem," muttered the driver, as he sighed with relief and pulled out of the lot and away from the partying bikers.

There was a little controversy at the boarding ramp when the employees of the company couldn't get a clean head count. They had 147 tickets but they were sure they had counted 165 people on board, but by the third time they tried counting heads they realized it was impossible, and the boat departed.

A throaty roar filed the air as the twin GMC diesel engines fired up and the turbo chargers kicked in. The captain signaled to cast off the dock lines, and using the bow thrusters swung the boat 180 degrees in is own length. Once the bow was pointed out of the small marina, he gave it 1/2 throttle and headed out into the channel.

He kept it at 1/2 throttle as he cruised past the Queen Mary and then swung to the starboard and headed across the Long Beach Harbor. The traffic was light and by the time he was clear of the commercial anchorage, he was up to 10 knots. He headed slightly northwest through the Harbor and inside the breakwater to get as much smooth motoring as he could, and then turned to the Port and left the harbor at the Los Angeles Lighthouse.

The San Pedro Channel was pretty calm and there were 4 to 5 foot swells spaced very far apart. It made the 120 foot boat roll a little, but not enough to be uncomfortable. She got up to her cruising speed of 22 knots and settled in, while the partyers did their damnedest to drink the bar dry.

On the aft deck, a bunch of girls were dancing to the music being piped over the speakers, and much to the enjoyment of the guests and crew, a couple of them started to strip. It was normal for them to do since most of them worked at *Shipwreck Joey's* back in LA, which was one of the nicer nudie bars.

Matt was the bouncer at Joey's, and he was acting as master of ceremonies and wardrobe assistant. As the girls would take off a piece of clothing they'd hand it to him. He would smile, and then throw it over the side. A trail of clothes followed the boat almost all the way to Catalina.

On the bow Treb, Dick, and Rom passed a bottle of Southern Comfort and a joint.

"Well Bro, you gonna miss this kind of life or what?" Rom asked.

"Why should I miss it?" Dick looked at him hard.

"In case you didn't notice, you're getting old and you just got married."

"Who you calling old?" Treb smiled, "I ain't no older than you, and I can kick your ass just like always."

Dick started laughing and passed the joint. Treb saying he could kick his ass had always been a standing joke. When it came to fighting there was no one who could beat Dick.

Dick Bondano and Treb had met thirteen years earlier in a bar fight in Las Vegas. Treb had come into this small bar just off the strip while he was riding across country. About five or six very large truckers had decided they wanted to see if this big biker could handle a whipping, so they jumped him.

Dick had been sitting at the bar nursing a three day drunk after getting fired from his job, and he relished the idea of a real kickass brawl. He watched as three truckers took turns on the big man, and soon he could see the biker really didn't need much help, but he wanted in, so he jumped in with both feet.

At 6' and 180 pounds, Dick wasn't all that large, but his Hawaiian ancestry gave him a mean look, and he was wiry as hell. Besides that he had been raised in a martial arts family. His father, his grandfather, and all of his uncles were Masters in Filipino Kali, the ancient art of weaponry. Dick had been trained since childhood in Kali and Jeet Kun Do. After Vietnam, martial arts were his life and he had worked as an instructor at Bruce Lee's old school, the *Jeet Kun Do*

Academy .

Later in life he decided to opt for a little less violent occupation and ended up in Las Vegas working as a guard at a chemical company.

As he waded into the fight beside the large biker on that day thirteen years ago, his life changed.

Ever since then, they had been inseparable friends. They rode around the country for awhile and then settled in the south bay area of Los Angeles. Treb had opened a gym and Dick had gone back into martial arts with a vengeance. Now at 38 years of age, he owned a martial arts school in Torrance and was a coach for boxers and wrestler's as well as teaching his real life love, kickboxing. Whenever things would start to get to him, he'd enter the ring as a sparring partner and let off steam.

It had always been a joke between Treb and Dick that Treb could kick his ass. They both knew it wasn't true and laughed about it.

"Ok," Dick laughed, "so when did Karen say you'd have to sell the bike?"

Treb laughed and swung at him haphazardly. When Dick caught his hand they tumbled to the deck, rolling and laughing like a couple of kids.

"Hey, come on you guys!" Rom laughed, and he started to pour Southern Comfort over the two on the floor.

Dick's hand flashed out of the jumble and pulled Rom's feet out form under him. In a few seconds there was 750 pounds of biker in a pile with Southern Comfort adding to the sticky mess.

Just then Karen and Daisy came out onto the bow. Daisy was Dick's current girlfriend.

"Hey, come on guys, don't break him. I might need him tonight," Karen said.

"Yeah, Daisy added," and I could probably find a use for that filthy half-breed too." Referring to Dick's mixed Hawaiian ancestry.

Karen grabbed the deck washdown hose from the bulkhead and turned on the water. In a few minutes there were three large wet bikers pulling two shrieking wet women into the pile. They were all laughing so hard they didn't hear the loudspeaker announce the arrival to Avalon Harbor on Catalina.

People watched in a combination of awe, fear, and loathing as the *Catalina Express* pulled up to the pier. On the bow there was a pile of people wrestling, and on the stern there were eight to ten dancers naked as jay birds and undulating to sounds of Steppenwolf's "Born to be Wild".

In a few minutes the bikers piled off the Boat. The men were all covered in wet Levi's and smelled like a brewery which had just exploded. The girls were wearing nothing but very skimpy bikinis, as Matt had thrown most of their clothes overboard.

They walked, strolled, and staggered to the first open bar, the *Twin Palms*, and in a matter of minutes were as at home in the resort community of Avalon as they would be in the waterfront bars of Long Beach or the sleaze taverns of East LA.

Bob Bitchin

5

Being the law on a small island was usually a pretty mundane job, and Bob Fox was just the man to fill the slot. He's seen enough action in his life, and at 63 years of age he felt he had earned a little rest and relaxation.

The position of Sheriff was almost an honorary title on Catalina. Since there were less than 4,000 permanent residents, there wasn't a lot to do during the off season, and during the tourist season the parks and recreation department handled most of the area on the island.

Catalina's main draw was always the beauty and it seemed that everything he knew about "his" island led to the same conclusion. It had been a tourist trap from the day the first white man set foot on her back in 1542.

Fox kicked back stretching his 6 foot plus frame out in his comfortable chair and put his sharkskin cowboy boots up on the desk. He put his glasses on the desk and folded his hands behind the back of his head and once again started to daydream. In recent years that had been his major pastime.

He tried to picture ol' Juan Cabrillo landing at Avalon with his two little caravels some four hundred and fifty years earlier. How did it look back then? He knew Avalon Harbor had to be about the same shape, but it was still a mystery where exactly the Chumash Indian Villages were.

Cabrillo had named his newfound island La Victoria.

A few years later another Spanish explorer named Vizcaino landed in La Victoria, but he didn't have the same feeling for the people there as Cabrillo did. He described them as being ingenious in pilfering and concealing. He thought of them as thieves. It never entered his head that these simple people didn't know what it meant to own something. If there was a small boat on the shore, and they needed to use a boat, they used it. It wasn't theft, just communal ownership.

It was pretty well known that Catalina had been one of the lesser populated Islands of the Channel Islands group. The Islands off the coast of Santa Barbara were the centers of the Indian population, with the capital, Liyam, on Santa Cruz Island. There the mainland was a scant 15 miles from the islands. Catalina was over 20.

Only a handful of indians lived on or visited Catalina. The Chumash would paddle across the channel from Palos Verdes (The Green Hills) in their 25 foot plank canoes. These visitors would only spend a small amount of time here searching for shellfish.

Emerald Bay

The northern Islands of the Chain, Santa Cruz, Santa Rosa, and San Miguel were the centers for the Indian culture. Even though there were only about 1,000 Indians in total living on the Islands, there were an estimated 15,000 living on the mainland.

And the Chumash weren't the first occupants. Over 4,000 years before them the Gabrielino Indians occupied the islands. Catalina looked new to those who visited, but in actuality it had been continually occupied for almost 5,000 years.

What made the Channel Islands such a populous place was the wealth of the sea life found in the channel between the mainland and the islands. A hydrographic phenomenon known as upwelling enriched the fertility of the channel by constantly replenishing the surface of the Pacific with plankton. In the spring, billions of sardines would feed on the plankton wile spawning, and move inshore as the weather cooled off. Larger fish would then feed on this bountiful supply.

With this wealth of easy food, the Indians had a pretty easy life.

Even later, in the 1800's, the islands were still used more for recreation than anything else, but recreation of a little more violent type.

In 1818 the French pirate Hypolyte Blanchard was one of the last real pirates to enter the area, and he landed in Emerald Bay to replenish his food and water after being run out of Santa Barbara. He had tried to sack the wealthy Ortega Ranch near Monterey and was beaten back. Then he stopped near Santa Barbara to replenish his supplies when he was jumped by a party of soldiers. He just didn't have any luck in the area, so he decided to head south to San Diego. Unfortunately he needed supplies so he stopped at Catalina.

Little was ever recorded about his stay in Catalina,

45

but there have been shallow graves discovered on top of the hill in the bay, and from the clothing and other articles found, they were definitely from that period.

Blanchard was reported awhile later sailing to San Diego, but his ship never arrived there. It became another legend.

In 1598 a Spanish galleon hit Bird Rock just off the Isthmus and sank an estimated $2,000,000 in gold and artifacts and in 1852 another vessel went down with over a million in bullion. These treasures laid under the sea for many years, but they were finally discovered by divers in the popular diving area around the islands.

It was around this time the Indians found otter pelts were valuable to trade with the ever increasing white man. Daily, hundreds of canoes would head out in the search for these furry little animals. With small villages dotting the islands.

Then the more violent Russian seal hunters came. They had a particular like for the Indian women, and while they were killing off the otter population, they were pretty much doing the same to the Chumash population. Killing the men and raping the women.

The last traditional Chumash ceremony was held on the mainland in 1870.

It was much earlier when the Chumash disappeared from Catalina, and in 1846 the island was deeded to a sea captain, Thomas Robbins. It passed through a lot of people including the Wrigley chewing gum family before it was taken over by the Catalina Island Company, who owns it to this day.

The island of Catalina is a paradise to those who visit and it is the most visited of all the Channel Islands. The Channel Island group actually consists of eight islands. Four of the islands, San Miguel, Santa Rosa, Santa Cruz, and Anacapa are grouped off the coast of Central California. The remaining three are scattered

Emerald Bay

off the coast of Southern California. San Nicholas Island sits the farthest from the California coast, about fifty miles off, and is the least frequented. Twenty four miles closer to land sits the smallest of the islands, Santa Barbara Island. The farthest south is San Clemente Island. San Clemente is a military reservation and is rarely visited.

The one thing that all the islands have in common is a vast number of caves. Some, like Painted Cave on Santa Cruz Island, have been tourist traps since the days of the first Indian occupants, with an 80' entrance leading back almost a mile into smaller caves and back rooms.

Other caves are well below the water line, and have never been seen by man. All the time new ones are discovered by the many divers who frequent the area.

The earthquakes that keep Los Angeles jumping also cause problems on the islands. Since the islands are located at the end of two continental plates, they are actually always moving, and someday they will be part of Alaska if left unhampered.

Catalina has almost a million people a year walking her shores. The location of the island makes it a paradise. The strong north-west winds that blow down the coast of North America form Alaska are channeled by Point Conception, out around the inner coastal waters of Southern California. The phenomena is called an eddy, and accounts for the weather. In addition the four islands hat are grouped there further shield the inner coast from the winds making the weather almost ideal. Sitting in the middle of the area is Catalina, just 20 miles form the tip of Palos Verdes, one of the most exclusive areas of Los Angeles County.

There is a definite season on Catalina, owing mostly to the fact that the Californian is a spoiled breed. With good weather almost year around, they only go out when the weather is perfect. If it gets below 70 degrees they stay at home. This makes Catalina a summer place. During the winter it is almost deserted, but during the summer it is wall to wall boats. With almost a million boats located within less than 100 miles, and very few place for them to go, the harbors are full as long as the weather is good. To add to the influx of people, there are fifteen or more boatloads a day brought over by express boats out of Newport Beach, Long Beach, Redondo Beach, and as far south as San Diego.

Most of the year Catalina has a constant north-west wind blowing down the California coast. In the summer it is a warm sea breeze that keeps the temperatures on the island bearable. In the winter it is biting and cold and only the residents of Avalon, a very few hearty sailors and a skeleton crew on the rest of the island remain.

During the transition, in late May and through the month of June, you can never tell what the weather will do. Heavy fog, strong winds, hot sultry days, and bone chilling cold can all happen in a week.

Fox's reverie was interrupted when he heard the sounds of someone walking up the boardwalk in front of the office. He sat up and put his feet under the desk, putting his glasses on as if he were working. It wouldn't do to let folks know how he daydreamed all the time.

6

Mia Albey walked into the Sheriff's office and sat on the corner of his desk. Fox couldn't help but admire the way she fit into those tight white pants. It was the uniform for sheriff's deputies on the Island and Fox wanted to thank whoever designed them.

Mia was 24 years old and had been working on the island for almost three years. She had come over on vacation while living in Redondo Beach and fallen in love with the place. If the term "California Girl" were in the dictionary it would have her picture next to it as an example. She looked like all the ads for suntan lotion you had ever seen.

She had long blonde hair, a good tan and one hell of a body.

She'd been working at Classic Motors, a car lot off the pier in King Harbor and it didn't take long for her to decide on a change. In a matter of weeks after she'd visited Avalon, she had quit her job and came back to the island with a small bag of clothes and nothing else.

It only took her a day to find a job at *The Twin Palms*. That night she was carrying her tray of drinks like she'd lived there all her life. The way she filled her "uniform" and her friendly attitude brought in big tips. The uniform for The Twin Palms consisted of tight pink short-shorts and a tight white T-shirt with twin palms pictured in a very prominent place.

It was a little while later that Mia learned how Catalina worked.

Winter came.

Now winter in Southern California is pretty mild compared to the rest of the world, but the community of Avalon goes into hibernation anyway. The summer population disappears back across the channel and blends into the mainland, leaving only a skeleton crew and a few die hard residents.

When the Twin Palms started to lay off employees for the shorter winter hours, Mia started to worry. Then one day it came. The manager called her upstairs into the office.

She thought she knew what was coming and was ready for the layoff.

But she was wrong. It seems that the manager didn't want to lay her off, he wanted to lay her, period.

By the time she managed to get out of the office she had a torn T-shirt and was crying.

And that was how she met Sheriff Bob Fox.

It was almost two and a half years since that manager had been sent packing off the island, and just as long since Mia started as the Sheriff's helper. She did her job well, was honest, and as it turned out, she had a real feeling for the job. She started as a kind of secretary and office helper. In a few months she had the office running smoother than it ever had before. The reports were all filed and the place was cleaner than it had ever been.

Besides that it did his old heart good to have her around the office. He could understand why that manager had gone off the deep end over her, but he still didn't condone it.

After awhile she started to help him on the heavier traffic days out in town. Now she was his chief deputy. In the past couple of years she'd attended security schools during the winter over on the mainland and had gotten into the martial arts pretty strong. She commuted to the mainland, a one hour boat ride, two times a week. For awhile he thought maybe she had a boyfriend over there, but he found out she was simply going to her karate classes.

Sheriff Fox shook his head as if to clear it, and spoke, "So how goes the battle out on the streets?"

Mia smiled at him a little longer then the time needed to be courteous. There wasn't anyone on Earth she loved as much as this old man, and she knew he'd turn her over his knee if he heard her call him that. He was the father she never had, and more than that, he was her mentor.

"Same old bullshit, boss," she smiled, "just a new load of tourists off the 1 o'clock boat and a couple of big wigs who came in on their yacht having too much fun. One of them thought I was a waitress in my uniform and pinched me. Boy was he surprised when I started to arrest him."

He waited for her to say something about the uniform being too "sexy" again, and when she didn't, he asked her, "Why didn't you bring him in?"

"It was too much fun watching him trip over his tongue trying to explain what he was doing. Poor old guy could hardly talk by the time I put my handcuffs back in their pouch. I don't think he'll ever live down being busted by me in front of his guests. Seems one of them was a Superior Court judge from Los Angeles, and the old coot was drunker than a shrimp boat captain on Saturday night."

Fox could picture it all going down and he smiled, more to himself then to Mia.

"Hey kid," he started, "how 'bout watching the office for a minute? I wanna run across the street for a second and get one of those shrimp cocktails for lunch."

"Ok," she said, and winked at him slyly, "but watch out for them old partyers, they go for those white pants on lawmen.

He steadied himself on the desk as he rose from his seat, letting the slight dizziness go away. Lately he found the dizzy feeling coming a little more frequently and lasting a little longer then it used to.

Mia hid the look of concern on her face by the time he looked up at her. She knew how bad he'd feel if he thought she was pitying him.

But it wasn't pity. It was love in the purest sense.

She swung off the desk and down into his chair.

"Be right back," he said, and disappeared out the door of the office.

Mia glanced around the familiar surroundings and felt a feeling of warmth and belonging. It was the first time she could remember actually belonging somewhere since her mother had died. From the night of that automobile accident until she met Bob Fox she had never felt really wanted.

Oh, she'd been used a lot, and she'd even used some people, but the real feeling she sought had only been found here in this little office, on this little island.

She glanced from the door Fox had just left by over to the coffee pot. As always it was half full, sitting on top of the file cabinets. There were four, three drawer cabinets with a board laid across the top of them forming a table. That was the nerve center of the Avalon Police Department. All police matters were first discussed for hours on end over massive cups of coffee. Fox's favorite beverage, and, as he often said, his only remaining vice.

The rest of the office consisted of two desks, two phones, and a makeshift holding cell. Nothing fancy, but to Mia it was home. It was even more of a home then the small apartment she lived in, and there were times when she wondered why she even kept the place. She worked, ate, and slept at the office, only going home to change clothes and shower.

Once again her mind wandered to Bob Fox. She dreamt repeatedly about finding someone like him only closer to her age. There were even times when she was willing to forget the age difference, but fortunately Fox reminded her. She knew he loved her also, and not like a daughter, but not like a girlfriend either. It was different. Just like he was. Different. There was an honesty about him, and something else. Even though she trusted him completely, she felt there was a part of him she would never really know. Something from the days in his past.

In the two and a half years she had known him he'd talked very little about his past. She knew he had been a bomber pilot in "the Big War", as he always referred to World War Two. He'd also told her about how, after the war he remained with the department of Army in Europe, but he was real vague about his job there. Just something about working with the old underground during resettlement in Eastern Europe and then in Central America. He was with the predecessors of the CIA, and stayed with them through the transition and founding of the current CIA. That was all she knew.

When he returned to the United States he went to

work for a large electronics firm. Once again his job was classified and all she knew was he traveled all over the world and worked with a lot of very strange people.

And then his last "job" before retiring in Catalina.

He was a private detective in the South Bay area of Los Angeles. This was the life she could picture him in. This big loveable gray-haired man standing well over six feet tall and never weighing less than 225 pounds, taking his cases of troubled kids, women, and the underdog. That was her view of Sheriff Bob Fox. A knight.

Her knight. Her knight in shining armor.

Her reverie was interrupted was interrupted by the door bursting open.

"Mia, you gotta get over to the Twin Palms." It was Babs, one of the waitresses that lived full time on the island. She and Mia had gotten along pretty good, but she'd never seen her like this.

"What's up Babs, trouble?"

"Well if there's not, there soon will be."

"Why?" Mia asked, trying to calm her. "What is it? Is there a fight?"

Babs bent forward and rested her hands on the desk, She looked real nervous.

"There a bunch of bikers that came into town on the two o'clock boat. They were drunk when they got here and are getting drunker." She took a couple of deep breaths, and then continued.

"They already threw out a couple of customers and broke the jukebox," she continued.

"Phillipo's pretty scared, and sent me over to get the Sheriff."

Phillipo was the manager that took over after Fox had the old manager thrown off the island. She could picture him being scared. He was a pretty small guy and scared of his own shadow.

"Ok Babs, let me get the Sheriff back here and I'll be right over."

"But, maybe the Sheriff should…" Mia's look stopped her in mid-sentence. Babs mumbled something about being sorry, and headed out the door.

Mia walked over to the door and looked across the street to the seafood counter. Fox was deeply involved in conversation with Norm Quient, the owner. They spent hours talking about the only thing they had in common. "The Big War."

Sometimes the stories would go on forever, so Mia waved until Norm saw her. He turned the Sheriff around and sent him back across the street.

As he came in she was strapping on her baton and he knew something was up.

"Sheriff," she hesitated for a minute, then started again, "Bob, there's a little trouble at the Twin Palms. I'll go over and settle things down. I'll be right back."

She had tried to make it sound unimportant because if he thought it was dangerous he wouldn't let her go. More than that, she was afraid if he went he might get into something he couldn't handle.

He looked a little disoriented for a minute, and then mumbled at her to go ahead on.

"Yeah, ok, you can handle it. I'll be here if you need me." And he went back to his chair. She heard it squeak in its old comfortable way as he kicked his feet up on the desk.

Bob Bitchin

7

Phillipo Farrell came out from the back room at the Twin Palms with another two cases of Coors from the walk in refrigerator. He was having a hard time with them like he always did. He just wasn't built for carrying heavy shit. Once again he cursed his small stature as he started transferring the cold beers into the beer cooler.
"Hey Mack," he heard form the far end of the bar, "hurry up with those brews."
Phillipo looked up and tried to smile.
"On its way," and he took a couple over to the guy.
He was starting to think this day wouldn't end. It wasn't ten minutes after he came on shift that these

bikers came in, and they looked like they were there to party non-stop. It wouldn't bother him so much if they didn't scare him so much, but in reality he was close to panic.

He saw Babs come back in and knew the sheriff would be there soon. He felt himself relax a little. The sheriff was old, but he could take care of himself. Phillipo didn't know if he could handle all these guys, but that wasn't his problem. He got paid to do the dangerous stuff. Phillipo didn't.

He heard a beer bottle break over by the pool table and turned to see what happened.

Two of the biggest guys in the place had another monster up on the pool table and they were pouring beer all over him. He thought of what the felt on the table would be like when it dried out, but decided against saying anything to them about it.

"So you think married life will be fun, huh?" Rom said, as he dumped an ice cold beer over Treb's head.

Phillipo tried to hide behind the bar as he saw Mia Albey come through the door. He felt the same yearning he always felt when he saw her. Then he wondered why she had come instead of the sheriff.

"Hey Babs," he called to the waitress standing a few feet from him across the bar, " I told you to get the sheriff. What's she doing here?"

Babs just ignore him like she always did. He hated the way most people took him for a piece of furniture, and vowed someday to get even with them. The women in particular.

Just as Mia came through the door Treb reached out and grabbed Dick's hand and twisted it up behind his back, shoving him onto the floor. Dick had drank enough beer to slow down his reflexes just enough for Treb to get away with it. Then Treb put his feet against Rom's large stomach and gave a hearty shove, slamming him against the wall.

The noise from Rom's collision with the wall scared the hell out of most of the people in the bar. The resulting crash from the gift shop next door could be heard as their little souvenir ashtrays and sea shells fell from the shelves. Rom had hit the wall hard.

Mia looked over to the disturbance and waded right in. One of the first things she had learned about law enforcement was never to show fear and to always take the initiative.

She was halfway across the bar when she noticed that the three guys in the fight by the pool table were huge.

Oh well, she thought, I can't back down now, and she went to the guy wearing the Levi jacket who was laying on the floor below the pool table. He was busy pulling on the biggest guy's arm.

She reached out to pull him to his feet and grabbed him by the arm.

The next thing she knew she was flying through the air and landed next to the big guy who hit the wall a few seconds earlier. As she dropped to the floor her leg fell across his lap where he lay in a bundle on the floor.

Rom felt the leg before he saw it and thought it was Treb's forearm. He grabbed it and gave it a good natured twist to show that he was down, but not out.

Mia felt the leg start to twist and thought it would break if she didn't do something quick. She shot out an open handed jab to the big man's carotid artery just below where his skull met his neck. He collapsed instantly.

By this time Treb had gotten off the pool table and was walking over to help Rom get up. It was then he saw some strange girl in white give Rom a judo chop and drop him.

He didn't know who she was, but even though he was kind of in a fog he knew he had to help his friend. He reached down and grabbed the girl by her hair and started to lift her off Rom. Before he knew what was happening she'd grabbed his arm, twisted herself around it until she was straddling it, and started kicking him under his jaw.

He was so shocked he didn't fight back. He just stood there with this wildcat on his arm, kicking him in the face.

About this time Dick made his way around the pool table and took hold of the girl in white. She twisted and released her grip on Treb, dropping to the floor, landing on her feet like a cat and twisted around trying to land a spin kick. Dick's reflexes took over at this point, and he blocked the kick using his left hand to push the foot around to knock the girl off balance.

Mia spun the foot through the kick as she had been taught, and lifted her hand while still in the spin, trying to land it against his face as she spun through.

Before it landed Dick had it blocked with his right.

Then she started throwing ever punch she knew, as fast as she could throw them, acting out of sheer instinct. Each time it was countered.

It lasted only a couple of seconds but to Mia it seemed an eternity. Each punch was thrown almost by reaction, and each one was blocked as if the whole thing had been rehearsed.

Pretty soon her head started to clear and she started to feel something she hadn't felt in a year or more. Fear.

No matter what she did she couldn't land a punch. This guy really knew what he was doing. Whatever move she tried, he was there to counter the attack. It was as if he could read her mind.

Then, as though through a fog, she started to hear laughter.

Who the hell's laughing? she wondered. She jumped back, pulling out her baton, and realized the answer mid swing.

Emerald Bay

It was Dick Bondano, her instructor from the Academy of Martial Arts.

He grabbed the baton in mid swing and popped it out of her hand, coming around with it stopping just an inch from her head.

He was smiling.

"Ah, grasshopper," he said in his best imitation of his television counterpart on "Kung Fu". "Does not the bull facing north fart to the south?" and he started to laugh.

Soon the whole place was laughing, and Mia's shame was overcome by the humor, and she soon joined into the laughter too.

Dick was one of the reasons she continued to commute to the mainland. Not only was his the best school in this part of the country but he was one of the best instructors in the field. Besides that, she liked him.

She looked at him now, standing in front of her. Somehow the biker standing in front of her just didn't fit the image of the clean cut, well mannered instructor. She was used to seeing him in his white Gi and the sterile environment of the Academy of Martial Arts. It didn't seem possible that this could be the same man. His dirty Levi's were old and faded and hadn't seen the inside of a washing machine in months. This was topped off by a black T-shirt. The words "Sex, Drugs, and Rock and Roll" were proudly printed across the front, and just below the statement was the name of the establishment that sold it. *Hermosa High* in Hermosa Beach, over on the Mainland. Sounded like a high school, but it was a head shop. The crowning piece of this ensemble was a Levi jacket with *Oahu State Prison* emblazoned on the back. This just didn't seem like the same man she'd held in such high esteem back at the academy, but she was glad to see him just the same.

Then she remembered why she was in the Twin Palms in the first place.

"Dick!" she tried to sound stern, "What the hell are you doing tearing up my town?"

His boyish smile was infectious and any attempt at being stern went out the window. He walked over to Mia and gently took her by the arm, guiding her to a barstool out of earshot from the crowd.

"So this is where you disappear to after class," he said. "I wondered why I never saw you anyplace but at the academy. How long have you been over here?"

She could feel the same thing she had always felt since she'd met him. A warm glow deep inside, and the smile that came over her face could no more be stopped then the ocean's tides.

"I've been here a couple of years." She looked down and picked her fingernails like a child being found doing something wrong. "It's kind of a hideaway and the first real home I've had in years."

She didn't know why, but she felt she had to explain her actions. Besides that, Dick always made her feel like a little girl.

Then she remembered once again why she was here.

"Dick," once again trying to look stern and failing," what's going on here? You gotta get these guys outa here before Sheriff Fox comes down here."

"We're not worried about any hick sheriff," Dick said. "My best friend just got married and we came here to party. Screw the sheriff!"

Mia could see he was pretty well into his cups. She started to worry then. She would have a real hard time trying to keep Dick and Sheriff Fox apart. It would be like having her brother and father fight, only her feelings for Dick weren't exactly brotherly.

The thought wandered around in her head while Dick wandered off the barstool and back over to the two big guys he had been wrestling earlier. It was the first time she really noticed the other guys. Both of them were big, but in different ways. One was large and kind fat. He had to weigh in at 300 pounds or more. He reminded her of a character out of the old underground comic strip "the Furry Freak Brothers". Fat Freddy. This was the one they called Rom.

The other guy was big, but big in another way. He was well over six feet and it was obvious he was in damn good shape, but there was more. There was almost an aura about him that stood out visibly.

Dick pulled the larger of the two over to where she was sitting.

"Mia, this is Treb," Dick held the man's hand like a paw and put it into hers, "Treb, this is Mia, the girl I was telling you about the other day."

The big biker held her hand for a second and mumbled something, but she couldn't hear a thing.

The girl I was telling you about the other day!

The statement hit her like a thunderbolt. She thought he didn't know she existed except as a student in his class. Why was he telling his friends about her?

"Yeah bro, you were right. She's a fox...," the large man slurred his words a little,"... but you didn't tell me she was a girl scout."

Just then a couple of other bikers came up behind the big guy and pulled him around to face them, slapping a pitcher of beer into his hand. He drank straight from the pitcher, and in his hand it just looked like a very large glass.

A very attractive blonde wandered over and kind of melted against Treb.

"This is my ol' lady.." he hesitated for a second and then smiled, "..I mean my wife, Karen. Karen, this is Mia.'

Mia looked at the girl. She was small, extremely pretty, and her face had an openness to it that made her feel like she already knew her.

Treb went on.

"Hey babe, remember the mystery girl Dick was telling us about? The one that was in his school an' kept disappearing? Well this is her." Then a big smile swept over his face. "This is sheriff Mia," and he started laughing like it was the funniest thing he'd ever heard.

Karen smiled at her and said "Hi," holding out her hand. "Don't mind this ox" she gave him a nudge, "he's wacked out of his gourd. He's ok most of the time."

After they shook hands the little girl turned on Treb and seemed to grow two feet taller.

"Listen, this is my honeymoon, and I'll be damned if we are going to spend my honeymoon night getting drunk in some sleazy dive with your old riding buddies.!"

He looked around the room like a small child, then held his hands palm up and looked at her.

"What am I supposed to do? These are my friends."

"I really don't give a damn what you do, but I'm gonna be naked and in bed with someone by midnight."

Even though they had been together a while, the mental picture of her laying next to him almost sobered him.

"Ok," he smiled a boyish grin, "midnight."

The noise of a breaking bottle came from across the room and Mia looked up to see Phillipo being pulled across the bar by one of the bikers. She got up off the stool and started across the room.

Before she got halfway to the trouble spot she heard a voice bellow out behind her. It was Treb.

"Ok you assholes, this is my party and my rules. No fuckin' over the bartender and don't make any goddamned trouble. I sure as hell don't want to spend my wedding night in a fucking cell, and the pig's on this island are friendly. Let's keep it that way. Anyone wants to fuck around's gonna have to start with me and Dick."

He hesitated for a little bit and a smile spread over his face.

"Let's make that, anyone who wants to fuck around will have to start with Dick. I'm saving my strength for tonight," and he grabbed Karen around the waist and lifted her like a rag doll.

Mia walked back over to the bar where she had been sitting.

"Thanks Treb. I don't want to stop your party, but I have my job. Thanks for your help."

"Help hell. I was serious," he smiled. "This bitch may kill me tonight. She told me we've just been practicing for this night the last two years. If that was practice I may need to call in help at midnight.

He was cut off by a glass of beer being poured over his head by Karen, and then she sauntered off like a pixie. He watched her as she walked away and Mia could see the big man was as in love as a man could get.

"Say," Treb asked Mia," where could a guy get a car to take a little drive around here? Maybe if I took her out for a little drive around sunset the rest of these crotch rocketeers would head out of here?"

Mia thought for a minute, then smiled.

"There's an old powder blue El Camino parked in back. It belongs to the ex-manager here. He kinda left it here when he left and I've been driving it. Why not take it?" She stopped and thought again, and then continued. "Just turn right out of the parking lot and follow the road to the end of town, then follow it up the hill. It will take you along the road to the small airport on top of the island and all the way to Emerald Bay if you want to go that far."

Treb said, "That's great!"and wandered off to find

65

Karen.

A few minutes later he was back, with Karen hanging on his arm and Rom breathing down his neck.

"You sure this is ok?" He looked at Mia.

"Sure. No problem. Just don't wreck it, it's not insured. By the way, don't tell the Sheriff it's not insured," she laughed, "He'd kill me!"

Treb turned to Dick.

"Hey brother, Karen and I are going up the hill for a bit, and Rom insists on going to take pictures and keep us out of trouble." At this Treb made a face as if to say "Who needs this shit!"

Dick knew Treb couldn't say no to Rom, no matter what he wanted. They had been through to much together. He smiled as the three of them headed out the door with Rom swinging his camera behind him and grinning like a Cheshire Cat.

Dick poured himself another glass of beer out of the pitcher in front of him and looked at Mia. She looked better in her uniform then she did in her workout gi, and she looked damn good in that. He figured after all the time he'd wasted already, he had better do something soon or he'd never forgive himself.

Mia was having the same thoughts, and for a minute their eyes met.

Dick took Mia by the hand and started leading her away from the group. She didn't know if she should follow or pull back, so she just followed. He led her through the bar and out the door. Soon they were walking across the street to the beach. She wanted to say something, and at the same time, didn't. She wouldn't have known what to say anyway.

When they reached the sand Dick stopped and sat down on one of the wrought iron benches that decorated the strand. He pulled his motorcycle boots off and stuffed his socks into them. Then he rolled up his pant legs. She just stood there like a little kid watching him.

He took off his Oahu State Prison jacket and pulled his T-shirt over his head.

She couldn't take her eyes off him. The way his lean body rippled with each movement. He was like a panther. His body was hard and tight and each movement was as if choreographed.

Mia was in another world as he held out his hand again and hers fell into it. They walked across the soft white sand to the waterline, and then led her slowly along the beach.

As they walked under the pier he stopped and leaned against one of the pilings. It was beautiful. The sun was setting behind him and everything seemed to happen by rote. His arms opened, she floated into them, and they kissed.

Bob Bitchin

8

Al Huntington looked out the window of the '64 Motor yacht *Disappearance* and saw they were about to come in to Emerald Bay. He had never been on the island before, but he recognized the *Rogue* sitting at anchor in the small and picturesque Bay. He had chartered it a week earlier and had it brought over and left here just for this meeting. He'd told the charter company he was going to stay on board for a week, and then they could pick it up and sail it back to Marina del Rey.

The meeting had been arranged very carefully. The man from Costa Rica, El heffe, would come in by sea plane to a point 60 miles off Catalina. A sailboat would be waiting there for him. He would transfer to the boat and they would then come in to Emerald Bay. Meanwhile Al would come in on another boat, the *Disappearance*, which he had chartered as if her were a tourist. The last two members of the meeting, Armando and Jose Tirantia would come in by the Catalina Express boat. For some reason Tirantia wanted it kept very quiet about his being with them. He didn't want this *El heffe* to know he was here. Said it would be better for Al in the long run. The plan was to meet on the *Rogue* after sundown. They were the only boats in Emerald Bay, and since it was not a weekend and the season hadn't started yet, the odds were pretty good it would be left alone.

He hit the intercom button and talked to the skipper, learning they would be on the mooring in thirty minutes.

He walked out onto the rear deck of the yacht and saw Eva laying in the sun on a large platform mattress made just for that purpose. She was wearing a suede "butt floss" bikini bottom. It covered a little in front, and disappeared into the crack of her ass. Al liked the new suits. She wore no top and looked like she had nothing on at all as she lay there. Her firm rounded behind was covered with oil and well tanned from the sun. Al walked over to where she was and sat on the edge of the platform, resting his hand carelessly on her firm butt.

This is the way life will be from now on, he thought. This will be my lifestyle. Yachts, beautiful women, and all the money to do it with.

His hand moved softly on Eva's rear, massaging it slowly. He slid it down between her thighs and nudged her legs slightly apart. Absentmindedly he continued to massage her soft, nether cheeks, and the warm sun combined with the erotic massage started to arouse him.

Emerald Bay

Just as he reached her hips to untie the strings on her suit, he heard the intercom.

"Sir, we are about to pick up a mooring. In what area would you like to stay, the center of the bay or off to one side?"

Al looked down at the inviting sight below him, and then shrugged.

Business before pleasure, and he got up and walked forwards and up the stairs to the navigation deck. The Captain was at the wheel and the crewman was busy tying on a bow line out on the forward deck. The navigation station looked like something out of Star Wars. There were digital readouts all over the console and more overhead. In the background of the engines strong rumble were the sound of at least two marine radios, one constantly telling the weather conditions and the other with a garble of sounds that Al couldn't make out. The captain's hand rested on two chrome levers with red knobs on them. They had just come around Indian Rock and were heading past the *Rogue*. As he eased the levers back the engines sound subsided. The boat slowed as they passed between the empty mooring cans bobbing in the crystal clear green waters that gave Emerald Bay it's name.

He didn't think it a good idea to tell the captain of the chartered boat his reasons for being here. As far as the Captain and crew were concerned this was just a pleasure trip for he and his girlfriend.

The Captain and his crewmen were busy picking up the mooring buoy and shutting down the boat's navigational equipment. The other crew member, a shapely redhead named Allyn, was busy behind the bar.

"Would you like a drink, sir?" she looked up and asked.

"Yeah, make it champagne, very cold," he smiled.

Yeah, he thought, I could learn to like this life.

Allyn brought him his drink, and as she walked away he watched her long legs and firm behind dance beneath the Tahitian styled Pareo she wore. Then he glanced out the window.

About two hundred feet away was a large sailboat that looked as if it had seen years of service at sea. Her hull was easily 70 feet long and she was schooner rigged. On the top of the fore mast was a square topsail. *Stone Witch*, *San Francisco* stood out stark and white against the black hull.

On deck he could see a large Latino. The same one that made drinks when he was at Armando's home. He knew that somewhere on that boat was the man he was to meet, *El heffe*, and he wondered who he was and what he was like.

The sun would soon be setting and the meeting wasn't scheduled until midnight, so he had some time to kill. He walked into the main salon and sat back on the overstuffed sofa. He picked up the remote control and flipped the open switch. A panel started to raise and behind it was a rear projection television screen almost five feet across. He pressed the button marked *Tape One* and the movie *Rambo III* started to play. There were three other tape buttons, and all he had to do was flip a switch and his choice of movies would come on the giant screen. Everything from Walt Disney's *Fantasia* to the original *Deep Throat*.

When the Captain was through with his duties he walked into the salon.

"Will there be anything else, sir?" he asked.

"Yeah. Two friends of mine are coming in on the 5:45 boat that comes from Long Beach. Could you see that they are picked up?"

"Certainly sir," the Captain said with a smile. "Would you like to go, or can you tell 'em how to recognize them?"

Al thought for a second. Instead of having to go with

these peons to meet the boat, he'd just send Eva. She knew both of the men that were coming in, so why not.

"You go and get the shore boat ready," he said. "I'll send the girl in with you."

And then as if an afterthought, "and take the other crewman with you, there may be luggage."

Al had a thought in the back of his head that maybe he could get his hands on that bartender broad if everyone else was off the boat.

He walked out onto the aft deck and slapped Eva on her bare butt cheek.

"Hey, go with these guys and meet Armando and Tirantia at the Catalina Express. Bring 'em right back here to the boat." He looked at her for a second, " and put some fucking clothes on , you look like a whore."

Eva was used to him talking like that and she ignored it. She wandered off the deck and through the salon, to the forward stairway. She liked being on a boat, and loved this one. As she went down the curved stairway she let her hand rub along the mahogany walls. They were like silk to her. A far cry from her childhood home.

She entered the master cabin and looked around. It was hard to believe she was on a boat. The massive cabin had a king sized bed set in between two carved teak bedside tables. The walls were teak and varnished to a high shine. At one end of the cabin was a closet with siding mirror doors. They had an ingenious little catch at the bottom to keep them from sliding while at sea.

She looked in the mirror as she unwrapped the towel from her body. All she had on were the skimpy bikini bottoms.

She thought, "I'm glad my mother can't see me now," and then she smiled and felt good. Her mother was back in Guatemala and owned a large general store in their small town. Each month Eva had gotten Al into a good mood, usually just before sex, and got him to send her money.

Eva'd learned a lot in the past four years. She'd learned the power of sex. She'd learned how to use her body, and she'd learned to what extremes men would go for a pretty girl. She vowed to use her looks and her body to make her mother as comfortable as she could be. Then she would escape this life and move home to Guatemala.

She'd learned, in a word, how to use love. But she had not learned what it was. Not yet.

Eva pulled off her bikini bottoms and stepped into the shower. She let the warm water run over her body for a about five minutes, then stepped out and toweled herself off. She knew she was going to pick up the man she had seen at Armando's house, and she knew he had power over Al.

She also knew she had power over him. She saw it in his eyes. A strange look. Questioning. Almost as if he knew her.

She put on her tightest shorts and a halter top. She stood and looked in the mirror. It was just the look she wanted. Her dark skin was even browner with the sun she had gotten today, and the lime green short skirt fit so tight she could see the outline of her womanhood. The halter top was white, and her large dark nipples could be see if you looked hard enough, and she knew he would look hard enough.

She put on some perfume and ran a brush through her dark black hair. Then she went up the stairs.

The Captain and the crewmen had the small boat ready and Al was deeply involved watching Rambo single-handedly wipe out the Russian Army on the giant screen TV. Eva walked over to the girl behind the bar.

"Can you make a margarita on the rocks for me,

please," Eva asked, trying to be friendly.

"Certainly madam," the girl replied coldly," would you like white or gold tequila?"

Eva looked at her and could tell that the girl didn't like her, but she didn't know why.

"Gold, please," she said. This time with a large smile, trying even harder.

In the four years she had been in America she had not had any girl friends. She never had a chance to meet any women, and the few she did meet were usually older. In four years she had only met one or two girls her own age and they were with dealers who had come to see Al on business. The girls had their noses so far into a bag of cocaine they didn't even know where they were. Besides that they were obvious in their dislike for Eva.

She didn't know they were jealous. She didn't know they were jealous of her lifestyle, of her looks, of her innocence.

And with Allyn it was even more. Allyn once had the chance to lead the life Eva was living, and she eventually opted to live on her own and earn her own way. She had no respect for this girl-child living in a woman's world. There was no way Eva could have known that.

Eva took her drink and went down the gangway, completely oblivious to the way the Captain and crewman stared at her. Soon the motor was started and the twenty five foot Boston Whaler was headed across the mile and a half of coast to Isthmus Cove.

It was a fast ride to the pier where the Express boat would land. They got there about twenty minutes before it was due in. The crewman tied the Whaler to the dock.

"We might as well have a drink while we wait," the Captain said as he took her hand to help her onto the dock.

There was a small bar a little ways up the beach so the captain and Eva headed there, leaving the crewmen to tend the shore boat.

They took a couple of stools at the palm covered bar and ordered two margaritas. As the girl behind the bar was making them, Eva looked around. The bar itself sat in a little patio attached to a restaurant. The place was almost deserted and they were the only two on the patio. A small dirt path led north to a small store that sold picnic items and suntan lotion to the tourists, and behind the bar she could see a dirt road winding up the hill. A blue El Camino was coming down the road leaving a wake of dust in its trail.

She watched as the truck turned off the road and towards the bar, almost hitting the phone booths there. It pulled up behind the bar, and three people got out.

A small blonde girl walked out onto the patio holding the hand of a big guy dressed in Levi's and a black T-shirt. He looked a little toasted, and the other guy, even heavier, was just plain drunk. The drunk kept taking pictures of the other two.

9

As Treb walked up to bar he looked at the two people sitting there. One was dressed in the white uniform of a charter boat Captain, and the other was just plain unbelievable. He felt Karen's hand tighten on his until he stopped staring. The girl was a stone fox.

He pulled a chair out at one of the table on the patio and Karen walked over to the bar to order their drinks. Rom came up and just stood there, staring. His mouth hung open and Treb was afraid he'd start catching flies if he didn't close it.

"Hey, Rom. Rom!" he poked him, "Sit down for Christ sakes. What the hell, haven't you ever seen a woman before?"

Rom just stood there. Treb kicked him in the ankle. "Sit down, damnit, you're starting to get a hard on standing there," and Treb laughed.

He glanced back at the bar and had to admit it was hard to take his eyes off her. As he watched her, she turned around on her stool and looked over at him. He couldn't believe how pretty she was.

You better get hold of yourself boy, he thought to himself, this is your fucking wedding day, and no time to start eyeing other women.

As Karen headed back to them with the drinks, he glanced away from the girl and started talking to Rom.

"Hell of a ride over here, huh Bro?" he asked.

Rom just kept staring.

"Hey, Rom, you gonna be Ok?" Treb asked.

Rom just mumbled something as Karen put drinks on the table and sat down.

"What's the matter with him? He sick?"

"No babe, I think he's in heat," and he indicated the girl sitting at the bar.

Karen looked over at her.

"Well, I guess she' ok if you like the type," she said, her claws coming to full extension.

"Obviously the boy likes the type," Treb said, indicating the semi-stupor Rom was in.

Karen picked up her drink and took a swig, not taking her eyes off the girl at the bar.

"Ok, let's see what we can do," and with that she got up and walked to the bar.

Karen liked Rom and wanted to help him out, but her underlying motives weren't so pure. She knew that if Rom was with this girl, Treb would never go for her. It was one of those rules bikers tended to take pretty seriously. Besides, she could almost feel Treb trying to avoid looking at the girl. They'd been together a long time, and she knew when he was in lust.

Emerald Bay

Karen walked over to the girl. She had to admit she was attractive. She looked young, about her age, and that made it easier.

"Hi," she held out her hand," my name's Karen. You staying on a boat out here?"

Eva was surprised. She wasn't used to people just coming up to her. When Al was around they usually kept their distance. She was taken back for a minute and didn't know what to say. The Captain spoke first.

"We're on a boat over at Emerald Bay, around the point there." He indicated a jetty of land north of the bay. "We're here to pick up some people." He looked over at the El Camino, "Do you live here?"

By now Eva realized that it must be normal to speak to people in bars. She smiled at the girl who was standing there.

"No, we don't. We're on our honeymoon. Got married this morning," Karen said still looking at the girl.

Eva joined in. "Which is the lucky man?" she asked, looking over at the table. Before Karen answered she knew the answer.

"The one with the 'Fuck the World' T-shirt on," Karen said, hoping the words would shock the two at the bar.

Eva looked at the girl with envy. Married. A normal life with a husband and a home. She looked back at the girl standing there and realized this was the first time since she ad come to America she wasn't being watched by one of Al's henchmen.

"I was just going to find the lady's room, "Eva said, "would you help me find it?"

Karen was taken aback this time. The girl actually seemed like she was trying to be friendly. By the way she was dressed, and with an obvious paid crewmen sitting there, she figured she was just another hooker or spoiled rich kid. Either that or someone's toy. In

79

any case she looked like someone Karen wouldn't like.

Eva got up, and the two girls walked off the patio together. Two fisherman who had just come in were walking up from the pier, as the girls passed them they both swung around like a pair of swinging barroom doors. They were paying so much attention to the two girls swinging rear ends they both missed the step, falling flat on their backs. Everyone in the bar started laughing.

As the girls walked down the dirt path to where the restrooms were, Eva started the conversation.

"Please don't think I'm strange, but I have been in America for four years and this is the first time I have met someone my own age that I can talk with. I hope you don't mind."

Karen looked at her and inside she started to soften. Maybe she had misjudged the girl because of how she was dressed. Then she thought of how many times she had wanted to talk to someone and couldn't when she had been working at the massage parlor years ago. She thought of how she hated being judged by people because of how she dressed or lived. She looked at Eva again. The girl had an open look about her, and Karen decided she might have been a little premature in her opinion.

It was as if Eva could sense what was going on in Karen's mind, and before they entered the restroom she was talking non-stop about everything that she'd kept bottled up for the last four years. They were only gone twenty minutes, but it was the best twenty minutes in the past four years for Eva. She told Karen how she got to be with Al, and what it was like being in the cage he had built for her. Then she talked about the little things. Girl talk. She hadn't had anyone to talk to in so long that it just bubbled. Karen never said a word. She just listened, and the more she heard, the more she felt for this very pretty girl. Karen wrote her phone number on a matchbook and gave it to her.

As they came back down the path they saw the *Catalina Express* had come in, and Eva saw Armando and Tirantia walking towards the bar. She reached over and grabbed Karen's hand.

"Can I see you again?" she was pleading.

"Anytime you need me, just call. You have the number." Karen squeezed her hand back and they stopped for a minute and looked at each other. Karen put her arms around Eva and they hugged for a minute. When she stepped back she saw a tear in the girl's eye.

"Don't worry," Karen said, looking into her deep blue/green eyes," You have friends now." And she walked away feeling warm inside.

Karen walked to where Treb and Rom were sitting, and Eva went over to where the men waited. The Captain got up from the bar and paid for the drinks. He headed for the shore boat.

.....
"What the hell happened to you?" Treb asked, looking at Karen. "You were gone a fuckin hour," he exaggerated.

"What happened, you two fall in love or something?" Rom went on, tilting back his head and downing another margarita. Even though his head went back, his eyes never left the girl. This caused him to twist his neck and Karen was sure she heard it snap.

She looked at them for a minute.

"Yeah. Something like that," and she just smiled to herself.

Rom sat there in a stupor, his tongue lolling out of his mouth like it had a mind of its own, watching the girl's ass sway as she walked to the Boston Whaler with the three men. His head swayed back and forth with her hips. His tongue made like a windshield wiper on his chin.

"Does this mean I don't get to meet her?" Rom asked. It was obvious his heart was breaking. At this moment he looked more like a St. Bernard puppy than a man. His mouth hung open, his tongue hung out, and drool ran down his chin.

Karen looked at him with pure love. Rom was her best friend as well as Treb's. She reached over and wiped his face, pushing his tongue back inside his mouth.

"You'll meet her. She and I are friends," she said.

She watched as the small boat pulled away from the dock, and Eva was looking back, smiling.

"She's staying on a boat over at some place called Emerald Bay," she said, pointing north. "She said it was a pretty big boat. You guys want to drive over and check it out?"

Treb said, "Why not?" slurring his words slightly. It was obvious the point of him feeling any pain was long past.

In a few minutes the El Camino was bouncing along the dirt road, making full use of its minimal width heading from Isthmus Cove to Emerald Bay. Every once and a while the front wheel would get a little close to the cliff's edge, causing Karen to wince inwardly, and a bunch of rocks to go careening down the side of the cliff. Rom was so busy rolling a joint of some Maui pot he wouldn't have noticed if they had gone over the side. All it would have done would have been to wake him up from his daydream about his new found love. Karen was mixing some tequila and lime juice that she picked up at the store as they pulled out of the cove. She had missed out on the drink-a-thon Treb and Rom had enjoyed while she was in the ladies room with Eva. In twenty minutes they had downed 4 double margaritas each. She was oblivious to that fact. She was just cutting the limes with Treb's Buck knife and pushing them into the bottle. Treb grabbed the bottle and took a big swig.

"There," he smiled," now you can get some more limes in there."

Karen looked up at him. "Gee, thanks for the help," she laughed, and she continued to slip a few more limes into the bottle.

They came around a curve and there in front of them was Emerald Bay. It was beautiful.

From their vantage point 200 feet above the bay the water looked like a sheet of green glass. They pulled over in the middle of the road and got out, taking the bottle and the joint with them. The sun was just below the horizon now, and the sky was glowing an iridescent blue. Far off across the channel they could see the lights of Los Angeles starting to come on.

They staggered from the car to the edge of the cliff, and Treb caught Rom as he was about to try his luck at flying. They dropped to a sitting position at the edge of the road and just stared off at the sight below. Karen looked at the two of them sitting in the dirt, turned the bottle up and chugged down three or four ounces. Here's to our wedding day, she thought, and walked over to her men.

The three boats that sat there looked like they were flying above the bottom instead of sitting on the water. There was a reef just in front of the moorings, and it stood out clear and white against the blue the water painted the deeper parts of the bay.

One of the boats was all black and looked like an old pirate ship. It had two large masts and a yard arm to carry a square sail. The other sail boat was a little smaller but in much better shape. It looked to be deserted. The last boat in the harbor had to be the one the girl was on. It was a large motor yacht and they could see people moving about and the Boston Whaler tied up to it.

.....

On the boat Al had tried his move on Allyn and decided she wasn't worth the hassle. When the crew and Eva were out of sight he flipped on the X-rated movie on the TV. Then he told her to bring him another glass of champagne and one for herself.

Allyn had been working on the yacht for a year, and in that time she had learned to read people pretty well. Especially the men. This one was an open book. He was crude, obviously involved in some kind of underground, and a little scary.

"No thank you, sir," she replied, as she brought him his drink. "I don't drink while working."

"That's no problem baby," he said reaching for the glass, "how about a little blow?"

She stood up and looked at him.

Cocaine was the biggest problem she had in life. The problem being, she could never say no. For a couple of years it had dominated her life and it was only after she'd lost just about everything she cared for that she'd been able to give it up. Actually the only way she gave it up was to get the job on a boat, where she wouldn't be tempted as much as she was when she was a waitress in a bar.

And now here was this guy, leering at her and holding out an ivory vile to her. It had to hold at least two grams and she knew looking at him this was not cut. It was probably close to pure.

She hesitated, and then stepped back.

"No," she mumbled, more to herself than to him. "No, I don't do that anymore."

He arose form the sofa and walked to her, holding out the vile.

"Come on ... here take the vile. Keep it."

He was walking to her as she walked slowly backwards until she was against the bar. He reached around her and set the vile down on the bar. She just stood there, watching him.

His hand came up to her face and he ran it through her hair. Slowly he ran it down her cheek to her neck, following the curve of her shoulder. When he reached the knot where the pareo was tied he hesitated for a second.

Allyn came out of her trance. She took his hand from her shoulder and eased out from between him and the bar.

"Thanks, but no. I don't do it,' and she walked up the stairs to the Navigation station.

The man took the vial off the bar and put it into his pocket, shrugging his shoulders. Then he walked back over to the sofa and switched the movie back to Rambo. He liked to watch the violence, without experiencing the danger.

When the boat arrived back from the Isthmus, Eva was like a new person. She was bright and bubbling. She went to Al and kissed him, and he just stared at her as she walked away wondering what had happened to her. Then she walked through the salon and up the stairs to the Nav Station, and up the next flight of stairs to the upper sun deck. There was a large overstuffed beanbag laying against a bulkhead and she fell back into it, smiling.

In the last half hour her whole outlook had changed. Life was good. All it took was one person to listen to her. One person she could call a friend. She could hardly wait to get back to the house, when she could call her new friend. They would go shopping together, go to movies, and just talk. She had so much she needed to say.

She smiled to herself again.

Looking across the bay she could see the El Camino coming in to view, driving erratically. It was trailed by a cloud of dust. Every once in awhile it would get real close to the edge, throwing dirt and rocks down and starting small slides. It followed the narrow dirt road along the top of the cliff, and came to a stop on the top of the hill above the boat.

She saw the three people get out and weave over to the cliff's edge. They were pretty far away, but she recognized them and waved.

Al walked out on the sundeck just as she was waving at her new friends.

"Who the hell are they?' he asked in a mean voice. He was still a little pissed at the stuck up bar girl.

"Just some people I met when I was waiting for your friends," she said, and then added, "she's my friend."

He looked up and could see the three people getting out of the car. They were staggering. Obviously plastered. Just what I needed, he thought, a bunch of drunks coming around here and screwing things up.

"Well, keep them away from here. I got business!" and he walked back down the stairs.

10

Chuck Silvers headed his 20' Sea Ox north out of Isthmus Cove. He'd just finished a quiet meal at the cafe, and planned on making his final check of the coves before tying up his boat for the night. The Laker's game would start in less than an hour and they'd be playing for their third championship in a row. There was no way he'd miss that game if he could help it.

Chuck had been the Harbor Master at the Isthmus for 3 years, and he liked the ease of the no action job. His biggest thrill was sports, and he found he could receive not only the Los Angeles channels on his television set, but also he could get San Diego. Twice as many channels to watch, twice as many games. It was his heaven.

For 8 years he'd worked in and around the hustle and bustle of Los Angeles after moving from Chicago. He was still an avid Bear's fan, and he'd been in untold fights whenever Los Angeles and Chicago would be playing.

Ever since he'd lived on the west coast he'd managed to find one way or another to make a living, but that was all he seemed to do. Make a living. He never seemed to be able to get ahead. Then, one weekend he was fishing on his friend Bob Morton's boat in Emerald Bay. He fell in love with the place. Every chance he got he would come over, either with Morton or Scotty, another friend who had a boat. Even when the games were on, he'd pack his portable TV, and hit the bay.

After awhile he got to know the Harbor Master, Nick Crociani. Nick had been Harbor Master for over seventeen years as he worked on the Great American Novel. When it was finished he'd gone off to New York to find a publisher. Chuck jumped at the chance to take over his job. He packed up his few belongings on the mainland and was soon settled into the Catalina way of life.

Now, as he passed out of the protection of Cherry Cove he gave the Sea Ox a little more throttle and he could see the swells starting to pick up at Eagle Reef about 500 feet off Little Gieger Cove. As the boats speed picked up he pulled his Bears hat down firmly on his head. The water was only a few feet deep at the top of the reef, and white water could be seen breaking through it.

The sun had just set, so Chuck wanted to get over to Emerald Bay and back soon. In bad weather the Catalina Channel can be treacherous, and he could feel bad weather coming in his bones. He throttled it up a little more, and made his way towards Indian Rock in Emerald Bay.

As he came around the point into Emerald Bay he saw three boats. This was odd for off season. He was trying to decided if he should charge them for their moorings when he noticed three people up on the road at the top of the cliff.

He watched them for a second and then realized they must have been pretty wacked. One guy lurched for the path that ran down the face of the cliff and started to roll down it. The second guy started to slide down the path on his butt, and the third person, a girl, just stood there laughing watching the first two.

Chuck figured the first one would fly off the path and hit the bottom of the cliff, but before that happened he managed to grab hold of one of the bushes on the side of the trail and stop himself. The second person was soon at his side. He laughed to himself as he saw them sitting there in the dirt, laughing so loud he could hear them way out where he was. He watched as they climbed down the rest of the cliff, stumbling and trying to hold each other up.

The third person joined them at the bottom and they started to walk along the beach. Chuck continued on into the bay, deciding that he would collect for the nights mooring fees. As he cruised through the harbor he couldn't help but laugh as he saw the three drunken people walk to the end of the small beach, and then they walked right into the water. At first a little hesitantly because the water was so cold, and then they just dove in. They made their way out into the surf and started swimming.

He could see they had started out for the big power boat tied to a mooring near the reef, but in a couple of minutes they changed directions and swam over to the *Rogue*, closer to shore. It was pretty obvious they'd misjudged the distance and were to tired to make the trip non-stop. He doubted it was their boat they had climbed up on.

It was kinda cold to swim out. He thought they were from the Disappearance, which is the boat they seemed to be heading for, and he wondered why they didn't take their dinghy in?

He aimed the Sea Ox toward the farthest boat out, the big pirate looking ship, to collect for the night's mooring.

On his arrival there he noticed the people on board were acting a little strange. As he entered the harbor there were four men on deck, but as he approached three of them went below. Usually people who came in for the night were glad to see someone from the bay so they could ask questions about the shore facilities. After collecting fees from the *Stone Witch* he headed over to the Motor Yacht. He saw the third person climbing up onto the *Rogue*. It was definitely a girl. Even from the distance he could see how the water fitted her T-shirt to her body.

He collected the night's fee from the white clad Captain on the *Disappearance* and started over to collect the last fee from the *Rogue*.

He was about 100 feet from the boat and he saw the figure of the girl walk over to the front hatchway and try the door. Suddenly the boat turned into a huge ball of flame. Everything happened like he was watching in slow motion. The girl was lost in the ball of flame that erupted from deep inside the boat. The two guys sitting on the side of the boat were lifted into the air and also disappeared into the explosion.

The sound echoed through the canyon a second later echoing off the cliffs that surrounded the bay, and the blast of the explosion knocked Chuck flat in the Sea Ox with an invisible force, his head hitting the towing bar mounted at the rear of the boat.

The same force that knocked him down reverberated

down through the emerald waters with more force then had been felt in the bay for centuries. It was so strong that it shifted a large segment of the reef that lay just a few hundred feet away.

Bob Bitchin

11

Dick and Mia were walking up the beach toward the Avalon. She was really enjoying her time with Dick, and was trying to think of a way to extend his stay. She was pulled out of her reverie when her belt radio erupted with sound.

"Mia, this is Bob, come in."

She took the small radio from its belt holder and pressed the send button.

"Yeah, Sheriff, this is Mia, what's up?"

"There's been an explosion on a boat over at Emerald Bay. Chuck Silvers, the Harbor Master, was knocked unconscious for a couple of seconds. They've called for an ambulance. You'd better get over there and see what happened. The Coast Guard is on their way from Long Beach and I have the fire boat standing by waiting for you.

"I'm on my way. Two minutes." She hesitated, "Was there anyone on the boat?"

"We don't know yet. Get your ass in gear. Call me when you get there. Out"

"I gotta go," she said to Dick as she started towards the pier, "Will you be here tomorrow?"

"Yeah, I'll get a room and wait for you, Ok?"

She smiled and reached into her pocket throwing him some keys.

"Here, 37 Wrigley Street, small place in back, green and white," she smiled. "I'll be back as soon as I can."

He pocketed the keys and waved as she ran off, turning back to the bar. She saw him walk in and felt better than she had in years.

She ran the half block down Crescent to the pier. The two regular fireman and one volunteer were on the boat. As she jumped in they cast off and pushed the throttle down hard.

In a matter of seconds the boat was up on a plane and the twin out drives pushed the boat along at almost 40 knots.

They held their speed out of the harbor, their wake knocking boats around like driftwood. When they reached the open waters they had to slow down a little because of the choppy conditions. The boat sped around Long Point and in less than 12 minutes were passing the Isthmus cove, turning in past Indian Rock to Emerald Bay.

It was dark by now and the bay was empty except for a burning hull floating about 100 feet off shore. The fireman knew exactly what to do and in no time they had the pump going and a stream of water started to beat down the flames.

Mia looked around and saw Chuck's boat about fifty

feet away. He was sitting in the boat holding something white to his head. Mia picked up the mike on the VHF radio.

"Chuck, Chuck, do you read me, over?"

She saw him reach for his radio.

"Loud and clear." He looked over at her, "Do you have to shout? My head hurts. You guys got here pretty fast."

"Yeah. Are you Ok?"

"I'll be alright, but there were three people on that boat. I don't think anyone could make it through that blast, we should start a search"

"Can you handle the boat alright?" she asked.

"I think so. I'll come by and pick you up. You can handle the spotlight, ok?"

"Right. Let's do it."

She saw him start his engine with one hand while he held something to his head with the other. He pulled over by the fire boat and she jumped in, bringing the first aid bag with her. She figured the fireman would be too busy with the fire.

Chuck had a large cut on the back of his head and he was bleeding bad. She took the cloth he had and replaced it with a sterile cloth from her first aid bag, first dabbing some hydrogen peroxide on the wound. It didn't look too bad.

"Never mind that," said Chuck, "there were at least three people on that boat, I saw them, let's see if we can find some bodies."

With that he swung the bow of the boat towards the dwindling fire and they started to circle the derelict. Mia held the spotlight and he steered the boat.

As they cruised around Chuck started to gain some reality back. The concussion had affected him more than he knew. As his thoughts came back he looked around the bay.

"Hey, there were two other boats here. Where'd

they go?"

Mia looked around. The glow of the fire gave the Bay an eerie glow.

"There's no one here now. Why didn't they stick around and help?"

"I don't know," Chuck said.

"What did they look like? Can you describe the boats?"

"Better than that," he said, searching through some papers on the dash of the boat, "here are the mooring rental fee slips."

Mia picked up the radio and turned to the Sheriff's tactical channel.

"Sheriff Fox, Sheriff Fox, this is Harbor-2. Do you copy?"

Harbor-2 was the boats radio designation.

"I copy Mia, what's up? What's it look like? Do you need me out there?"

"Negative boss. The fires coming down. I'm on the boat with Chuck and he seems to be okay. A small concussion. Little bleeding. That's about it." She let that sink in, and then started again.

"Boss, there's something a little odd out here. There were three people seen on the boat just before the explosion, and there were two boats in the harbor. Now the boats are gone. Not a sign. I wonder why someone would leave an explosion like this without trying to help? They just left Chuck laying there in his boat unconscious."

"Do you have the boat names or descriptions?"

Mia looked at the rental slips.

"One was a 64' power boat. Name: *Disappearance*. Home port, Los Angeles. White hull, white topsides." She waited while he wrote it down.

"Second vessel, 70' square rigged topsail schooner. Name: *Stone Witch*. Home port, San Francisco. Black hull, White accent stripe. That's all we have. I think they should be checked out, if for no other reason then to see why they didn't render assistance and——"

"What's the matter? he asked. "Why'd you stop?"

"I'll get back to you Sheriff. I just spotted something."

She threw down the mike and shined the spotlight on what was floating in the water. As they got closer she started to get an almost sinking feeling.

It was a body. The body was wearing Levi's and a black T-shirt. They pulled next to it. It was floating face down. As Chuck turned the body over in the water she almost gagged.

The face had been almost blown off.

They tried to pull the body into the boat, but they couldn't do it.

"What are we going to do?" she asked, looking at Chuck repeatedly. "We can't just leave him here."

We're going to have to. Tie this to his belt," he handed her a small yellow pouch," then pull the string once it's attached."

She did as she was told, and the small bag inflated with air. It was a bright yellow marker buoy.

He could see the look in her eyes.

"Look Mia, he's dead. A little while in the water won't hurt him, and there may be others. Alive. We have to keep looking."

She understood. She picked up the spotlight and they continued their search.

By now some of the people from, the Isthmus had come up the road on foot and were watching from the top of cliff. The ambulance pulled in from Avalon and Mia could see the flashing lights as it came around the bend into view.

Then she laid the spotlight down and stared up the cliff.

"What's the matter with you?" Chuck said.

She just stood there.

"Hey," he took her by the shoulders," What's the matter with you? You ok?"

The ambulance's headlights were shining on the back of a car. A blue El Camino.

It was the car she had let Dick's friends use.

Then the black T-shirt of the floater flashed into her mind.

There were three people that were seen on the boat. Two men and a girl.

She turned to Chuck.

"Did you see the people on the boat?" she asked.

"Yeah, they swam out from the beach," he pointed to the base of the cliff.

"What did they look like, these three?" she didn't want to hear his answer, because she knew what it would be. He described Treb, Karen, and Rom.

Dick's best friends.

"Take me back to the body we found, quick!" She told Chuck.

He spun the boat around. She swung the spotlight until she spotted the yellow buoy and then they made their way to it. The fire was dying but there was still enough light to give the buoy an eerie glow.

Mia looked down at the body and tried to remember which of the two big men she met was wearing a plain black shirt. Then she remember the words "Fuck the World" emblazoned on the front of Treb's shirt.

"His name was Rom"

She picked up the mike. They were still on the Sheriff's tach channel.

"Sheriff, this is Harbor-2. Do you copy?"

"I got ya Mia, what'd you find?"

"So far we found one body. Dead. He was one of the bikers from the bar. All I know is they called him Rom. He is the only one we've found, but from Chuck's description I think there are two others out here on the boat. One was named Treb, And the other

was his wife, Karen. They just got married today." She waited for a minute.
"Sheriff," she said softly.
"Yeah, Mia, what is it?"
"Sheriff, could you go over to the Twin Palms. See if there is still a man there named Dick Bondano. About 6'1", 185 pounds, Hawaiian." She hesitated again.
"Is he involved in this?" the sheriff asked.
"He's here with them. A friend... and Sheriff, if he's not there, try my place, he'll be there."
The Sheriff didn't say anything. He just sat back and put the mike down.
"You get that Sheriff?" she asked.
"I read you. I'll get back to you," and he signed off.
Chuck took the radio and switched to the ambulance's tach channel on the radio. He told them to meet him at the bottom of the trail. Then he tied a line around the feet of the dead body and slowly pulled to the shore.
While they were pulling the body out of the bay Mia walked down the beach. She wondered why they were on that boat in the first place. She also wished she could be with Dick when he heard about this. He was about as strong a man as she had a ever met physically, but emotionally he was very sensitive, and she didn't know how he would take it.
Then she remembered her job. She looked up from the beach and started to turn back to the boat. Just as she looked up she saw something a little way down the beach.
"Hey Chuck, down here," and she ran towards the dark mass laying on the rocky shore.
There was another body laying half in half out of the water. His arm was outstretched on the rocks, and his fingers convulsed, pulling the dirt to him like he was trying to move. His other arm lay at his side, bent at

the elbow and once farther down, where there was no joint. On the back of his shirt, covered in blood, she could read "Hermosa High", and she knew what it said on the other side. It was Treb, and he was alive. She bent down beside him and shined her small flashlight on his face. He was pale white, in a state of shock. He reached out and grabbed her by the ankle.

"Karen," he screamed.

And then he passed out.

12

Allyn mixed another batch of margaritas and poured them into the glasses lined up on the bar. She was still freaked out over what had happened. It was all so fast that she still wasn't sure of what went on. One minute she was setting up a tray of hors d'oeuvres on the table and the next they were flying out of the harbor with a boat burning behind them.

The two newcomers sat on the large sofa deep in discussion. All she could think of was this had to be the worst charter she ever worked.

At the far end of the salon she could overhear part of an argument between the Captain and the man who chartered the boat, it was too loud to be ignored.

"I don't give a flying-fuck what the God Damn laws of the sea are." Al was shouting, "I'm chartering this fucking tub and I want to be back in Los Angeles in thirty minutes, got it?"

The captain just stared at him. He was fuming, but he knew his job hinged on how he handled this. The charter company cared more about pleasing their customers then they did about the sea lawyers that might come along later. He turned his back and walked up into the navigation station. Here he was in his element. The room was dark, with a faint red glow from the instrument lights. He ran his hands over the instrument panel like it was a woman, caressing the dials and gauges. He looked at the Furuno radar screen, it was giving off an eerie green luminescence. It was set to read a 24 mile range, and in it he could see Catalina Island moving away from their stern. Even though they'd just pulled out a few minutes ago, the boat was already seven miles into the San Pedro channel. 15 miles ahead he saw the form of the Long Beach breakwater on the screen. His Standard Horizon VHF radio was starting to crackle with radio traffic as they got closer. He sat down in the white leather chair in the pilot station and just listened, staring at his radar screen., It was almost like watching television.

Allyn entered the nav station and handed him a drink. It was JB and soda, tall, just the way he liked it.

"You know I don't drink when I'm working," he said to her.

"Well, working or not, you looked like you needed this. Call it medicinal purposes," a faint smile on her lips.

"You know, we shouldn't have left without seeing if anyone was hurt." He was talking more to himself than to her.

"Do you have any idea what happened?" she asked.

"No. The boat just seemed to explode," he said, and thought to himself, "Yeah, it exploded, but not like a propane or gasoline explosion. Those are quiet and mostly flame. This sounded like I was back in Nam."

He watched the radar screen and could see a small blip heading from Avalon. It must be a fire boat, he thought.

The blip of the boat that exploded was fading on the screen as he watched. The radar bouncing off the mast had been a strong signal, but it was obvious the mast had fallen. The signal was much weaker now.

"Can you tell if anyone is coming after us yet?" Allyn asked, a deep concern in her voice.

"No, not yet." It was the first time he had really thought about what he would say when they asked him why he had left the scene. There was no way he could justify it other than that he was ordered to leave.

They sat in silence for a few minutes watching the scene play out before them on the radar screen.

"What's happened to the other boat?" she said, pointing to the blip that had to be the large sailboat that was in the harbor with them. The blip was disappearing from the screen at the west end of Catalina.

"I don't know,' he kept watching the screen," it looks like we're losing the blip. That's odd."

By now the small blip of the fireboat had arrive in Emerald Bay. The blip of the fire boat pulled close to the blip that represented the harbor boat. They were starting to lose definition because of the distance away. Now they were over halfway across the channel. At 25 knots it would take them a little over 45 minutes for the crossing. It had been almost a half hour already.

In the main salon the two new arrivals had concluded whatever it was they were discussing. Al sat by himself out on the rear deck. This would have been his big break, and now, as if the fates had made a decision, all hell was going on.

"Why me?" He thought, "What did I do?"

As though they could read his mind, Armando and Tirantia walked out onto the deck.

"Al," Armando started, " what happened back there?'

Al sat there looking back towards the island, even though he could not see it anymore.

"I don't know. The boat just exploded. I don't know what caused it."

"Well, Al, Mr. Tirantia and I have been talking, and it seems a little odd to us that the explosion should happen on a boat that you arranged for, and only you and I knew about. Don't you think that a little strange?"

Now Al was starting to get worried. He had been so caught up in trying to figure out what happened, he hadn't given any thought to the fact that he might be a suspect. He thought fast.

"But Armando, Joe," he said looking at the other man. Their eyes were staring at him as if he were dead, "I was supposed to be on that boat during the meeting too. Why would I...? His voice trailed off.

Tirantia spoke up. "Where did you get that girl? How did you know who she was?"

Al was more confused than ever.

"What-I don't know what you mean! Who is she?" He was in a panic.

"You planned this, yes?" Tirantia reached into his jacket.

"You don't think I...? I wouldn't do that. You know that." He looked to Armando, "Armando," now he was pleading, "Armando, tell him I wouldn't...". Al held his hands up in front of him, as if to ward off an attack.

It was too late. By the time his hands were in front of him he saw the gun in Tirantia's hand. It was a military style .45 automatic with a short black silencer

screwed onto it. Tirantia's killer eyes glared.
  The first bullet hit Al in the stomach. When his hands dropped to hold where the bullet went in a second shot sounded. This one went into his forehead. The force of the .45 caliber hollow point pushed Al back against the rear railing of the boat. He hit the walkway hatch and fell. The sounds of the shots were drowned out by the twin Detroit Diesel Engines which were running at full power just a few feet below their feet. No one on board heard the shots.
  Armando and Tirantia walked over to where he lay. Al's eyes stared up at them, but they held no life.
  Tirantia quickly tied a piece of docking line around the body's waist while Armando walked to the side of the boat. He unstrapped the 65 pound Danforth anchor that was used sometimes as a stern hook. He tied the line to the anchor, and in a minute the body was over the side, sinking to the depths of the San Pedro Channel.
  Tirantia pointed to the deck washdown hose coiled in the corner of the aft deck. "Wash the blood off the deck," was all he said, and he walked inside the salon and took his drink off the table.

  Allyn had left the Captain in the Nav Station and walked up the gangway to the upper deck. She didn't want to go back into the salon because the grease ball who was chartering the boat might hit on her again and she really didn't need that.
  She walked to the back of the deck and stood there, trying to make out the island they' just come from. It was a clear night, but they were too far away to see anything.
  As she stood there she heard sniffling coming from behind her. It was the greaseball's girlfriend. Allyn hadn't seen her since she'd come back from picking up

the other two men, and after the accident she'd forgotten all about her.

She looked around and saw Eva laying on the large beanbag she'd been sunning on earlier that day. Somehow she just didn't look like the same person she was before. Allyn knew the signs of a kept woman, and there was no doubt in her mind this girl was the property of the greaseball. To her there was no justification for a woman to degrade herself that way, and she'd taken an instant dislike to the dark haired girl.

But now the girl was balled up in almost a fetal position, a pillow being crushed in her arms as if it were going to save her from something. Her back heaved with heavy sobs, but they were silent sobs. Allyn walked over to her. Maybe she didn't like Eva, but it was another human being and it was obvious she was miserable. Allyn sat down on the edge of the cushion, putting her hand on Eva's shoulder.

"Can I get you something? A glass of water or a drink?"

The girl only stared at her for a minute like she was crazy, and then pulled away.

"Eva," Allyn said as she remembered the girl's name, " do you want me to get Mr. Huntington for you?"

The girl started to cry even more. She was uncontrollable. Allyn just sat there beside her, stroking her shoulder, looking out into the dark sea. A few minutes passed and the girl's breathing started to return to normal. Finally Eva spoke

"There were people on that boat," she said.

"Are you sure? I didn't see anyone on that boat all day long. What makes you think someone was on board?"

"Do you remember when I went ashore?" Eva's breath was getting steadier, and she seemed to be talking in a trance. Before Allyn could answer Eva continued. "Well, I met some people while we were waiting. The girl was nice to me. She was the first girl I've met in the four years since I've been here and she said she was my friend."

All of a sudden Allyn felt guilty about pre-judging the girl. Maybe she had been wrong.

Eva continued still in her trance.

"They were coming out to visit me. I saw them pull up on top of the hill and park. They climbed down the cliff and started to swim out. I guess they got tired because they stopped on that other boat. Then it blew up. I saw them die. She was my only friend."

Allyn just looked at the girl for a minute. All of a sudden she seemed very young and vulnerable. The tears had stopped running down her cheek but the pathways were marked in mascara. Allyn reached in her uniform pocket and took out a handkerchief, dabbing at the girls' face. The girl just sat there, staring into space.

In a few minutes Eva slumped down in the beanbag again and was asleep almost instantly with her head on Allyn's leg. Allyn sat there and stroked her head for a little while, and then got up, careful not to disturb her.

"Captain," Allyn said as she entered the Navigation Station, " there were people on that boat."

He looked for a minute. "Are you sure? How do you know?"

She told him what the girl had said.

"Yeah, I remember them. Two bikers and a real pretty blonde girl. They were at the bar when we were waiting for the two new arrivals. The two girls hit it off fast."

"Were they from that boat?" Allyn asked.

"I sure didn't think so. In fact. No, they must have been from the island. They were driving. I wonder what they were doing out there?"

He looked up at his radar screen and flipped a lever

taking the range down from 24 miles to 2 miles. They were starting to enter the harbor at the San Pedro entrance to Los Angeles Harbor and he needed a little more distinction on the screen. The *Disappearance* slipped through the opening in the breakwater and headed towards their charter dock in front of Ports O' Call Village.

"You better get out on deck and get the dock lines ready. We're going to tie up in about 5 minutes," he said to Allyn, and his mind went into automatic as he started docking procedures.

Ally walked out onto the forward deck and picked up the starboard dock line. She hooked the loop through the eye of the cleat and tied it off, gathering the rest of the line neatly so it could be thrown to someone on the dock. Then she repeated the operation on the other side.

As she walked through the salon towards the back of the boat she saw the two new arrivals sitting by the bar. They had fresh drinks in their hands. She walked out onto the aft deck and hooked up the Port line. Then she went for the other one, but it wasn't there.

That's odd, she thought. I'm sure it was here earlier. She walked over to the dock box and took out a fresh line. By the time she had it tied on and coiled they were pulling to the dock. The Captain had radioed ahead and there were two of the dock boys standing by.

As usual the docking was perfect. The boat slid into the slip without touching either side, and then stopped right in place. She threw the stern lines to the dock boys and then walked back to the bow, throwing those lines down. By the time she was back in the salon the men were gone.

As usual she started working by rote. She gathered the glasses from the salon and aft deck first. Then those in the Nav Station. She put them all on the counter and started washing them. This had been a fairly easy charter, not many people to clean up after.

While she was cleaning up the Captain was busy shutting down the ship. They would leave it at the charter dock until tomorrow so the Dock Boys could wash it down, then he would move it over to its slip in Wayfarer's Village Marina.

Allyn was putting away the last of the glasses on the shelf when Eva came down the stairs. She had forgotten all about her.

"Have you seen Al?"

Bob Bitchin

13

At first there was just a kind of light, very bright and very far off. A strange euphoric state completely enclosed Treb's mind. It was as if he were floating in space, and he could see himself laying on a bed. Nothing seemed strange or odd to him. It was all very natural. There was no fear, no pain, and no wonderment. Just peace.

His view as looking down as if he were fifteen feet above the floor. He could see the whole room. Dick was sitting on a chair next to the bed and there was a woman dressed in white doing something over by a table full of strange looking instruments.

In his mind's eye his life could be seen, but it wasn't

flashing before his eyes. It was just there. The memories of his lifetime. Everything was crystal clear, and he was comfortable with it.

Then he saw another scene. A soldier laying on a dirt field, his horse standing near him. A tree fallen on the dirt near him. Another life became clear to him. It wasn't confusing. It was just there. Another life. One he'd lived before, and as with the life known as Treb, it was just as clear in his head.

A third scene. A long white beach. A body laying on the sand. Darkened by the sun and parched. His hair long and blonde. A small boat washed ashore nearby. The man is clutching a shield. Another life. Clear, distinct, and complete. He was a Viking. The life is there in his mind, and he knows a choice must be made.

His will decided. It was not a conscious decision. It didn't denigrate any of the past lives. On the contrary. Three times has he lived, two of them have been complete. His love for Karen brought him back to this one.

The scene in the hospital room became crystal clear. Then it started to get very bright until the whole room was bright with pure white light. The edges of the light started to dim, leaving a tighter and tighter circle of light getting brighter, as if it were concentrating at the end of a very long tunnel. Still there was no fear. Just a feeling of euphoria. Peace. He was coming home.

Soon the pain started to come through, slowly, as life started to return to the body of Treb Lincoln. The light faded until all was black. he tried to move but was unable to. His eyes were closed, and he was fighting to open them. Sounds started to fill his ears. It started as humming and soon distinct sounds came through.

.....

Dick watched Treb laying on the bed. He'd been there for about an hour. Every day since the accident he'd come to the hospital to see if anything had changed. It's been three weeks since the explosion. Treb had been in a coma ever since they found him on the beach.

"Hey, his eyes are starting to move!" Dick called to the nurse.

The nurse turned around and walked over to the bed taking Treb's wrist in her hand and looking at her watch. Then she checked one of the many dials on the table.

"His pulse is stronger and his brainwaves are becoming active," she said to no one in particular, then she picked up the phone by the bed.

"This is Nurse Martin in 317. You better get Dr. Ostriker down here, stat. It looks like Lincoln is starting to come out of the coma."

She replaced the phone in the cradle and turned to Dick.

"I'm sorry sir, but you'll have to wait outside."

The door opened as Dr. Ostriker walked in wearing a white hospital jacket. He turned to Dick and smiled, holding the door open.

"This is what we've been waiting for. Wait outside and I'll let you know as soon as there's a change."

Dick walked out into the waiting room and sat down on one of the orange naugahyde benches. He sat there for a minute, then got up and walked to the phone. He punched in a number.

"Mia, it looks like he's going to come out of it. Any more word on what caused the explosion?"

"It's getting weirder by the day," she said. "The divers know for sure that it was an explosive device. Probably plastique like they used in Vietnam, only it seems it was something even more explosive. Kinds like the newer stuff they're using in Central America and the Middle East. Also, they can't find any kind of detonator. They think it was a chemical detonator. That would explain there not being any pieces left laying around. Oh, yeah, one other thing. This adds to the weirdness."

"What's that?"

"Well," she went on, "you remember the other boat that sank off the west end? The big sailboat form San Francisco?"

Al thought for a second.

"Yeah, I remember. The *Stone Witch* wasn't it"

"Uh-huh. That was it," she said. "The *Stone Witch*, right, well it looks like that was no accident either. They think whoever was on board scuttled the boat. Not only that, it turns out the boat wasn't from San Francisco at all. Sheriff Fox got a read-back yesterday from the Coast Guards Documentation center and they don't have a *Stone Witch* registered out of San Francisco. In fact, there's none registered fitting that description anywhere in the country."

"Mia, how about the men from the *Disappearance*? Have they been able to find them yet?"

"No. There's more mystery there. The man who chartered the boat never showed up. Not at his house or anywhere. The police have been looking for him and his girlfriend but they haven't found either of them. No one on the boat saw them get off in San Pedro. This is real strange. They don't know who the two men were that met them on the island. It's real weird."

"And it's getting stranger. Look, are you planning on coming over to the mainland tomorrow?"

"Dick," he could hear her smile into the phone, "you couldn't keep me away."

Ever since that day on the island she had been coming over and staying with him every chance she got. She'd told the Sheriff she was checking facts with

Dick, but they both knew the truth. Ever since she'd run into Dick her personality had changed. She was sparkling. Even with the events surrounding the explosion, he could see she was in another world.

"Ok," he said. "I'll meet you after the class. We can get some dinner. Alright with you?"

"Sounds good. By the way, I've got a meeting with the divers this afternoon. I'll let you know if they found anything new."

"Great, see you tomorrow," he said and hung up.

It was almost 4:30 and he had a 5 p.m. class back at the Martial Arts Academy. He walked back over to room 317 and listened at the door for a minute. Then he opened it a crack and looked in. The doctor was standing beside the bed writing something down on a tablet. The nurse was injecting something into the intravenous tube that went from the bottle hanging above the bed to Treb's arm.

"Doc," Dick waited for him to turn around, then continued, "what do you think? Is he coming out of it?"

"Looks like he made it. You might as well go on. It'll be at least 24 hours before he'll be able to talk to you. Why don't you see me here tomorrow at this time?"

.....

Dick slipped into the front seat of his pickup truck and put the key in the ignition, giving it a turn. The 1961 Ford pickup fired to life as if it were new. He liked his truck better than his newer car. It was him. He'd had it for over 15 years and kept the engine and running gear in top shape. The truck body itself looked like it hadn't been washed since he'd owned it. As far as he could recall, it hadn't. the orange paint had faded to almost a rust color and the only decoration on the truck was the large Harley-Davidson decal in the rear window.

The truck pulled out onto Carson Boulevard and he blended into the rush hour traffic. Even on the side streets in Los Angeles traffic got bad between 3:30 and 7, and as he crossed the bridge over the Harbor Freeway he saw that it was bumper to bumper as far as he could see in both directions.

It only took him a few minutes to go the couple miles up Figueroa and onto Torrance Boulevard. Before he knew it he was turning into the parking lot of The Academy.

He walked into the building and looked around. The first room was a large one, with a boxing ring set up in the center. Along one of the walls were eight speed bags. Boxers worked these to build speed and rhythm. All were being used right now, and the noise from these filled the gym. Along the next wall were five heavy bags. Each had the word "Everlast" plastered across it. These were used to put power behind a man's punch. The boxers had a trainer hold a bag as they punched it, while the karate students let them fly free as they punched and kicked at them.

One of his instructors shouted to him. "You got a call from that girl over in Catalina. Numbers on your desk."

Dick said thanks and went into his office, picking up the phone.

Sheriff Fox answered the other end.

"Sheriff's office, Fox."

"Hi, Sheriff, is Mia there?"

"Who's calling?"

"Dick Bondano. Is she in?"

"Yeah Dick, hang on a minute. How's Lincoln doing?"

"Looks like he's gonna make it."

Dick could hear him out his hand over the mouthpiece. Then there was another click on the line.

"Dick," she said," I guess you got my message? I just

missed you at the hospital."
"Yeah, what's up?"
"Things are getting pretty strange around here. You remember that girl I told you about? The one that was on the *Disappearance* with Huntington?"
Dick said, "Uh huh, what about her?"
"Well, they found her. Actually Immigration found her. Are you ready for something real odd? Mexican customs caught her trying to sneak into Mexico."
"I thought they never checked anyone going that way. Did they find out anything?"
"That's where it gets interesting. It seems they were going to let her into Mexico when a couple of men from the US border station walked in and took her over to the US side of the border. That APB we sent out did some good. They recognized her and are holding her there for us."
"Did she say anything?"
"Only that she never saw Huntington after the explosion. He disappeared."
"Does that help fit this thing together?" he asked.
"Only this. It seems she saw and talked to Treb, Rom, and Karen about a half hour before the explosion."
He suddenly got excited. "Is there any way I can talk to her?"
"Well, you're not supposed to, but I'm flying over to the mainland in an hour to drive down and pick her up. Wanna come along for the drive?"
.....
It took just a couple of minutes for Dick to get someone to take over his Karate class and he was headed for the Long Beach Airport in his truck. Traffic was heavy, so he had time to think.
Everything was still a complete mystery three weeks after it all happened. All they knew was the three of them were on a boat, and it exploded. The two other

boats in the harbor pulled out. One of these sank and everyone except the hired crew disappeared from the other one. It was getting harder to find anything out.

He parked on the lower level of the parking structure and walked into the terminal. Catalina Air was coming in at terminal 4, so he walked over to the gate. Mia was just walking down the gangway as he got there.

She wasn't wearing her uniform, but there was no mistaking her. She had on a pair of Levi's that fit better than skin, and a white nylon jacket over a T-shirt. He couldn't help but think how good she looked.

As she reached the gate she put her hands around his neck and kissed him. Then they walked through the terminal hand in hand.

As they walked out to the parking area, Dick filled Mia in on Treb's condition.

"He's starting to come out of it, but he's still in pretty bad shape. It's amazing he's still alive. The doctors said it's just his will keeping him alive. He has a massive concussion, five broken ribs, and a broken collar bone. Both arms were broken. One of them in five places. His left leg is pretty bad. The femur is broken and so is the shin. The doctor says he'll be laid up for at least a year, maybe more."

She looked at him out of the side of her eye. "What's that mean really?"

He smiled. "Probably a couple of months, once he gets on his feet, if I know Treb."

They reached the truck and she stopped.

"I can't pick up a prisoner in this," she said, looking at the rusted hulk of a truck. "We'd better get a rental car. The sheriff's office will pay for it."

14

Eva sat in the holding cell at the border station and stared at the wall opposite her. The graffiti was bilingual and she read it without thinking. All she could think about was getting home, to her mother. To somewhere she could breathe.

Ever since that night in Emerald Bay she'd been hiding. She didn't know where to go. Al had disappeared from the face of the earth, and even though she didn't care for him, he was the only one she knew. After she left the boat she'd taken a cab to the house in La Puente, but there were police all over when she got there. She had the cab drive around for awhile. Finally she remembered Armando, and had the cab take her to his house in Truesdale Estates. That had turned into a real mistake.

Jose Tirantia was there and he all but carried her into the house. When she asked him and Armando what had happened to Al they just looked at each other and were real silent. They started asking her questions. Did she know why they were at Emerald Cove? Did she know who was on the other boat? Did Al talk to anyone else about the meeting? They kept it up for hours.

She told them she didn't even know it was a meeting. She thought they had just gone over for a holiday. She was surprised when the two of them had show up there.

No, she didn't know anyone on the other two boats in the harbor, except for the people who climbed onto the sailboat just off shore. She told the men about meeting Karen, and her husband Treb and friend Rom.

Tirantia seemed even more interested in her past, back in Guatemala. Did she know her father's name? Did she know where he was, or what he was doing?

The questions went on all night. By dawn she had fallen asleep on the couch.

The next day she was questioned some more. They wanted to know everything about Al's business and his acquaintances.

The third day Tirantia brought her into his room. He was very rough with her. Much rougher than Al had ever been. He ripped off her sundress, which was all she had left, and then threw her onto the bed. He had been drinking and dong a lot of cocaine all day. He entered her roughly and she thought he would never stop.

Sometime the next day Eva woke up in Tirantia's bed. She rolled over and saw he was gone. She went into the bathroom to shower and found his overnight bag. As she was looking through it for some deodorant, his passport fell out. Curiosity got the best of her. She opened it up. Inside she saw ten one hundred dollar bills. She took two and put the wallet back.

After four days Tirantia left. Eva still didn't know what to do so she stayed on at Armando's house. For some reason he never tried to touch her. He just ignored her. Sometimes he would buy her some clothes, and then they would go out for dinner, always where he was well known. When they would return to the house he would say goodnight and leave here to herself.

It wasn't until over two weeks later she discovered why.

He was gay. He was sleeping with his houseboy.

The next morning she left. She took a cab to the bus station and a bus to San Diego. She walked the 8 miles to the border, and started across. She still had $55 left from the $200 she'd taken from Tarantia's bag.
......

Eva woke up and shook her head. The sights and sounds of the cell brought her back to reality. She sat up and rubbed her eyes, looking around. She was still alone in the cell. In the hallway outside she heard voices.

"She's in here. I'll get her. You pull your car around the side."

A deputy walked in and unlocked the door to her cell.

"Okay," he said as he roughly put her in handcuffs, "they're here to get you. Let's go."

"Who's here?" she asked.

"Catalina Sheriff. They want to talk to you abut a double murder," and he took her arm, leading her down a long hallway.

Eva couldn't even think straight. Double murder?

Who? Who was murdered? There had to be a mistake.

The deputy opened a door and Eva was taken outside. She was led over to a white Ford with two people standing near it. They didn't look like police. The girl looked like an ad for the Southern California Chamber of Commerce, and the man looked like something out of a Bruce Lee movie.

The blonde girl took her from the deputy, taking her by the arm.

"Get in the back," she indicated the back door of the car, being held open by the other person.

She got in and hit her head as she did so. Then she sat back in the car and the cuffs dug into her wrists. She didn't say anything.

The two who were picking her up walked back to the doorway and signed a piece of paper on a clipboard, then they returned to the car and got in.

Dick turned around in his seat as they pulled onto interstate 5 and looked at the girl. She could have the answers he was seeking. All he had to do was find them.

"Where are we going?" she asked. She was starting to get scared.

Mia spoke first.

"We're taking you back to Los Angeles. There are some big questions to be answered about an explosion in Catalina."

"Who.. Who are you people?" she asked. She was even starting to stutter.

Dick watched her as she spoke. It was hard for him to believe that this innocent looking girl could be the key to who killed two of his best friends and put Treb in the hospital.

"This is Mia, she's with the Catalina Sheriff's office," he said. "I'm Dick. The two people who died were friends of mine. Do you know what happened on that

Emerald Bay

boat in Emerald Bay three weeks ago?"
Eva sat forward to keep the cuffs from cutting into her back and wrists. Things were happening too fast.
"I don't know what happened. I really don't, "tears were coming back to her eyes again. She was afraid and alone. "besides that, one of the people who died was my friend. My only friend," and she started sobbing.
Dick looked back at the girl with tears running down her face. She tried to wipe them away with her shoulder but she couldn't reach her face with the handcuffs on.
"Mia," Dick said, "pull over for a minute."
She looked over at him and then pulled to the side of the freeway.
"Let me have the keys to the handcuffs," he said.
"I don't know. We shouldn't..."
"Trust me, Ok. This girls' not a murderer, and I want to find out what went on out there. Give me the keys, okay?"
She handed them to him. He got out of the car and opened the back door. Eva was crying and the sobs were shaking her. He slid in next to her and turned her around, unlocking the cuffs. Then he turned to Mia.
"Have you got a handkerchief or some Kleenex?"
She handed him a small packet from her purse. She almost felt a pang of jealousy watching him dab her eyes softly with the Kleenex.
Soon the girl calmed down.
"What do you mean 'your best friend'? he asked her. "How did you know those people?"
For the next few minutes, as they drove down the freeway, Eva explained what happened that afternoon in Emerald Bay.
Mia sat listening. There was so much emotion in the girl's voice that she believed her. So did Dick. Either

the girl was an excellent actress or she was a very lonely and frightened girl. They both believed the latter.

Dick looked at Mia through the rear view mirror. He could see she agreed with his feelings.

"When did you eat last?' he asked the frightened girl.

"I-I don't k-know," she said, still a little shaken up. "What is today?"

Dick turned back to Mia.

"What do you say we stop and get something to eat? I could use a break."

Mia pulled off Interstate 5 at San Clemente and then found a family type restaurant. Dick got a table and Mia took Eva into the ladies room to help her clean up.

As they came out of the restroom and walked over to the table Dick was struck by the beauty of the girl. He knew by now that he was in love with Mia, but he was still effected by the other girls stunning looks.

"Looks a little better now, doesn't she?" ?Mia said, and by the look in Dick's eyes she knew she was right. She added, "Hey you're with me, remember?" and laughed.

Eva smiled for the first time in three weeks.

"What will happen to me?" Eva asked Mia.

"Well, right now they just want you for questioning. Actually they haven't got anything to connect you with the explosion except for the disappearance of your friend Huntington."

"Where were you going in Mexico?" Dick asked her.

"I didn't have any place to go here, so I was going back to Guatemala to my mother."

Somehow Dick couldn't picture this girl on a dirt street in Guatemala. Mia must have read his mind.

"Look, after we get up to Los Angeles and they finish questioning you they probably won't hold you, but they won't let you leave the country either. How about staying with me for awhile over on the island? Maybe we can figure out what happened to our friends with your help."

"Are you sure? You don't know me. How do you know you can trust me?"

Mia smiled at her.

"I know."

Dick reached across the table and took Mia's hand, squeezing it softly.

While Dick and Mia ate a couple of sandwiches Eva devoured a prime rib dinner. Then she had two pieces of apple pie for dessert, a glass of milk, and a chocolate milk shake. As she sat there finishing up Mia's French fries off her plate Dick summed up what they had learned.

"So this Al Huntington was in the drug business? The two men who came out to meet you must have been in the same business, right?"

Eva shook hear head in the affirmative, still chewing on the last French fry.

"And you didn't know anyone on the other boat?"

"No. We never talked to the other boats. Either of them," she said.

Mia got up from that table.

"I'll be right back, I'm going to call Sheriff Fox and see what he can make of this," she walked off towards the phone.

Dick looked at the girl for a minute.

"You were real close to Karen, weren't you?"

"Yes. We were going to go shopping and stuff when we got back to the mainland. She understood me. I know you can't understand it, but in just a little while we became best friends."

Dick thought back to when he'd first met Treb, in that bar back in Las Vegas so many years ago. They had become just as close, just as fast.

"Yeah," he smiled at her, "I understand it. It was the same way with Treb and me."

"Is he going to be alright?   He must miss her awfully."

All of a sudden Dick sat up straight in his seat.

"Oh my god," he said aloud," he doesn't know!"

He grabbed Eva by the hand and almost pulled her out of the booth. He threw the money for the check on the counter and dashed to where Mia was on the phone.

"Come on, damnit! He shouted at her, "we have to get to the hospital!"

.....

They'd dropped Eva off at the West La Sheriff's office and hurried directly to the hospital. By the time they were up to the third floor and at the door it was too late. The doctor was standing at the nurse's station and stopped Dick coming down the hall.

"He was getting stronger almost by the minute," the doctor started, "then the police came in to question him. I told them he was weak, but they insisted. Said it was a murder investigation and took precedent," he shook his head. "Precedent my ass. When they told him his wife was dead you could almost see the reversal with your eyes."

"I have to see him, now! Dick said, holding the doctor by both arms and shaking him.

"Ok, ok. It can't hurt. It doesn't look like he'll make it through the night," and he walked away, shaking his head.

Dick entered room 317 and left Mia sitting in the corridor.

An hour later Dick came out of the room.

He was smiling. He walked over to where Mia sat and almost picked her up.

"Let's go home. We got some heavy fucking to do," and he led her through the door.

15

The Grunt & Sweat gym was quiet when Treb walked through the door. He walked over and turned on the overhead lights. Then he flipped the stereo to KRTH and tuned in some oldies. They were playing Pink Floyd and he turned it up loud. In the dressing room he stripped off his street clothes and put on his sweats. Soon he was ready for his daily workout. He hadn't missed a day since he got out of the hospital. His first workouts were almost laughable, but he kept it up and his strength built fast.

The speakers were blaring as he came out of the office. The first thing he did was to go over to do some abdominal work on the Roman Chair. 100 sit-ups started every workout. Then crunches. By the time he finished his ab workout his blood was pumping strong.

They'd said it would take years before he would be as strong as he was before, if ever. They'd underestimated him.

When he'd started after he got out of the hospital he would do five sit-ups and have to rest for half an hour. His bench press was less than 100 pounds, and the pain was so bad after three or four reps he had to rest fifteen to twenty minutes between sets. He had to use an empty bar for curls because the pain in his healing collar bone couldn't handle any more weight than that.

Within a month he was doing a normal workout using steroids to help the healing process. The doctor had been using steroids for a long time to help patients heal. He'd almost forgotten the big business in underground steroids to body builders.

Treb had known enough body builders to know how to use them, and with the help of his doctor he managed the perfect dosage. The recovery was miraculous. So was Treb's determination.

He had just finished his first set of bench presses and was getting ready for his second. He was adding another 45 pound plate to each side of the Olympic bar. First he did a set of ten reps with 225 to warm up. Then a second set of eight with 310. After that he would do another eight reps with 400 pounds, and a final burndown set of fifteen reps with 135 pounds. He had learned the system years ago when he'd worked out with Kal Szkalak, a former Mr. Universe.

The first set he used a moderate weight to warm up the muscles. Then he would go for a heavy weight to build strength. Then would be the heaviest. This one built size as well as strength. Then the last set used a lighter weight with a lot of reps to burn off fat in the muscle and give him stamina. Treb had been building back up to it for the past three months. Ever since he got out of the hospital.

The warm summer air as drifting across the beach and in through the open front door. Twenty years in Hermosa Beach and he still loved it.

He thought of Karen for a minute. He laid back with her filling his mind and gripped the bar. The 310 pounds seemed light as he pumped and pumped, trying to get the negative thoughts out of his head. Each day the thoughts would come back, but now they were mostly good. He missed her, but he had finally come to the realization that having her for as long as he did was better than most men could ever experience. Then he thought about what Dick had told him in the hospital room three months earlier, and smiled.

He was sliding on another couple of 45 pound plates when Dick came through the front door.

"Hey Treb, what's with the light weights? On vacation?" Dick laughed.

"Yeah ya faggot, I was just setting it up for a woosie, and you're it."

Dick walked over to where Treb was standing and they embraced for a minute.

"And what the fuck's a 'woosie'?" Dick asked.

"It's what you get when you mate a wimp with a pussy!"

Ever since the accident Treb never took one minute of his life for granted. The thought of not being able to say anything to Karen or Rom before they died nagged at him. Sometimes at night he would lay there and try to relive the last minutes of his life, trying to remember what the last words they had were.

"Hey Bro," Dick said, "how 'bout after class tonight we head over to the island and see the girls. I'm suffering from that old Hawaiian disease *Lakanookie*" and he started to laugh.

Treb laughed along with him for a minute, and then agreed.

"One thing though," he added," I want to dive some in Emerald Bay while we're there. Ok?"

"Yeah, okay, if you want to, but you have to promise not to go and get all maudlin on me while we're there. Promise?"

"Ok asshole, now move yer butt and let a man get some work done here," and with that he picked up the 400 pounds and did his eight reps.

Dick smiled to himself. Three months ago Treb couldn't get 100 pounds off the bench. He had found an outlet for his frustrations. He looked at Treb almost awe struck. It was hard to believe that just a couple months ago he was an invalid. Now his arms and chest were humongous, and his whole body was alive.

"I'll see you in class," Dick said, "Don't be late or I'll kick yer dead ass!" and he headed out to his truck, laughing.

Treb finished his last full set and stripped the bar down for his burnoff set. It felt good to be back in the gym. It seemed to give his life meaning, a goal.

While he was setting up the dumbbells to do some flys he played the same game he'd played in his mind since he'd been back from the hospital. The Puzzle. He had o fit all the pieces together to win. And he would win.

There were still some pieces missing. They had to find them. He hoped that maybe this weekend would be the time.

All summer they had been going over to Catalina. Some time was spent just sitting around and talking, trying to find some small thing they overlooked, and other times they put on diving gear and went to the bottom of the Bay to look for clues to the explosion.

They had put together a kind of scenario, but it was

missing some pieces. They knew that Eva's old 'keeper' as they called Huntington, had probably set up some kind of meeting at Emerald Bay. They knew that Armando and Tirantia had come over for that meeting.

Then there was the boat. The *Rogue*. It had been chartered by Huntington from a different company then the one he got his yacht from., It was obvious he was missing something.

Also there was the vessel the *Stone Witch*. Who was on it and why did they sink it? Was it involved with this meeting? If so in what way?

He moved on to the next workout station. He had set the gym up so the guys that worked out there could work different body parts to their max before moving on. He had finished his chest and back. It was time for the arm workout.

Even though he had to press himself to finish each day, the arm workout was his favorite. It gave him a feeling of accomplishing something.

He picked up the chromed Olympic curl bar and started his warm up set. Ten reps with 125 pounds went fast, and he could feel the warm 'pump' that came to his biceps. Then he put on another fifty pounds. Slowly he curled the weight to his chest, letting it drop completely after each rep. By the time he finished eight reps he could feel his biceps starting to burn. He put on another two twenty-five pound plates and faced the mirror. He picked up the bar and his face contorted as the 225 pounds pulled against the strain of his arms. The pain felt good. He barely finished his eight reps and dropped all but 85 pounds from the bar. Then he started to pump until he couldn't move his arms anymore.

He had found a way to keep his life going, and weight training and martial art training were the key. From the day he was released from the hospital he had worked-out without fail, and each day he felt better.

His days spent working out with weights in the morning, running on the beach and swimming during the day, and at the Martial Arts Academy each night. He loved the dedication and discipline. During the beginning the dedication kept him from thinking about what he'd lost. Then the loss helped him get through it.

He sat down at the Scott-curl bench after setting up the weight bar. As he curled the bar up he looked at his biceps as they strained against the weight. They were over 20 inches. 4 inches larger than he had ever managed before. He was finally in a condition he liked.

He finished with a shoulder workout and then his legs, and went into the shower room to clean up.

For the rest of the day Treb was on the beach. He ran 8 miles and then went for a swim. After a large tuna salad for lunch he got on his bicycle and rode from Hermosa Beach to Venice, through Marina del Rey, along the bike path on the beach. It was about ten miles each way. The air cleared his head and by the time he was back in Hermosa he felt exhilarated.

It was almost time to head up to the Academy for the Jeet Kun Do class with Dick. This was the hardest part of his day. Before each class they would spend twenty minutes doing stretching exercises. The rest of the class was in their early twenties or even their teens. They could stretch their limbs like they were made of rubber. Treb had two obstacles to overcome in stretching. One was the damage done by the accident, the other was daily weight training sessions.

A lot of his elasticity had been lost while he was laid up. Some of it would never return. Mended muscle tissue isn't as resilient as the original. This made it harder for him than for the average person. Add to this his age, and there was an even bigger loss of elasticity. His daily weight training made it even harder because it built up his natural tendencies to fight against muscle stretching. He would try to stretch out mentally, but his muscles would fight every action.

Near the end of the stretching session he was watching with envy as one of the younger men there was sitting in a full split position, laying forward with his chin resting on the ground in front of him.

"All it takes is youth," he heard from behind him. It was Dick. The class was about to start.

Treb liked Jeet Kun Do and Filipino Kali and would have liked it even if Dick wasn't the instructor. He liked the feeling of releasing tensions. After the warm-up and stretching, the class would move onto specialized movements. Sometimes they worked with weapons like batons or nunchukas, and other times it was barehanded.

The thing that made Jeet Kun Do stand apart from the other styles of martial arts for Treb was the individuality of each person involved. Bruce Lee had founded the style, and his idea was that each person is different, so each man should seek his own level of competency.   There were no black belts or brown belts. When asked what rank he held, Bruce Lee stated he was Bruce Lee. That was his rank.

What this meant to Treb was that he wasn't forced to use a style. Treb was 6'4" tall and weighed close to 285 pounds. A style good for a 5' tall, 120 pound man wouldn't be best for him. There were no standing katas to perform that turned you into a automaton. At the end of each class there was a fifteen minute period where each member of the class would spar a one minute round with each of the members. Tall, short, slim or fat, they all fought and trained against each other. It was the closest thing to formalized street fighting Treb could fund, and that was what he wanted.

  The class started and once again Treb was lost in the discipline of Martial Arts.

16

The last Catalina Express boat of the night docked in Avalon at a little after 10 p.m. Mia and Eva were waiting at the dock as Treb and Dick came down the gangway. Most of the men getting off the boat turned and stared at the girls as they passed. So did a lot of women.

"Hey lady, you gonna arrest me or what?" dick said to Mia, as he walked up to her and put his arms around her.

"Damn right. Now get yer butt down to the jailhouse so I can strip search you!" she put her arms around his neck. "Welcome home," she added and kissed him.

Eva and Treb stood aside and said hello to each other. When Mia and Dick broke it up Eva gave Dick a kiss and Treb hugged Mia.

Mia stood back and held him at arm's length.

"Damn boy, you been at the gym too much. You're starting to get deformed," and everyone laughed.

Eva and Treb still felt strange around each other and they didn't know why. It was like they each reminded the other of the terrible afternoon they first met.

When Treb would look at Eva all he could think about was how Rom wanted to be with her. If the explosion hadn't happened they might be together now. In a way she was Rom's girl and Treb couldn't forget it.

For Eva it was just as bad. Treb was married to Karen. Even though she only knew Karen for a few minutes, as the time since then passed, she felt closer and closer to the dead girl. She loved and respected Treb, but not in the same way Mia and Dick loved each other.

They never talked about these feelings and probably didn't know why they felt uncomfortable with each other.

The summer night in Avalon was balmy. They could see across the channel to the lights of Los Angeles and it looked like a sparkling pile of jewelry. The four of them walked along the promenade from the docks. Mia lived a block up from the beach in the center of town. They all headed up the hill without talking.

Once inside the small house they separated. It had become almost a ritual. Whenever Treb and Dick came over to visit Treb would take Eva down to the Twin Palms for a drink. That would give Mia and Dick time alone.

"Eva, wanna go down and have a cold one?" Treb asked, smiling.

Eva looked at him and then the other two. "No, I

think I'll stay here."

The three of them looked at her, then she broke into a big smile. "what's a matter, you guys can't take a joke? C'mon shorty," she looked at Treb, " let's get outta here before they start here in the living room and embarrass us."

On the way down the street Eva and Treb walked slow.

"How've you been?" Treb started. "Everything going okay?"

"Yeah I guess. How about you?"

"Yeah. Fine. Just been working out and trying to get into some kind of shape."

She stopped and looked at him.

"Treb, in case you haven't noticed, you are in shape. You look ten times stronger than when I met you. Why are you driving yourself like this?"

He walked on and was quiet until they turned onto the Promenade.

"It keeps me going," he said. "I guess it's all I've got."

She took his hand and looked up into his eyes. They stood there looking at each other for a minute, but to each it seemed like hours. Then, as if a silent signal went off, they reached for each other. They stood in each others arms for what seemed like an eternity. Neither said a word. They just held each other tight, as if life itself would stop if they let go.

Slowly they released each other and stepped back. Eva could see tears in Treb's eyes. Here eyes were just as wet.

He said, "Thanks. I needed that."

The tension broke. They both started laughing and couldn't stop. They wrapped their arms around each other again, but this time they were both smiling. Nothing was said, but at that minute both of them lost the guilt they'd felt for being alive. For living when others died. All of a sudden they felt the burden they'd carried since the explosion drop away. They both felt free.

.....
  Mia had changed from her uniform to some shorts and a halter top before heading down to the Twin Palms with Dick. She felt good as they walked down the hill, and they're hands swung back and forth like a couple of kids.
  "What are we going to do about those two?" she said. "they act like brother and sister. What's the deal? Did that explosion do more damage to the boy then we know about?"
  Dick smiled at her. "No, he still has his marbles, it's just going to take some time."
  They turned and walked into the Twin Palms. Phillipo was behind the bar and saw them come in. He still lusted for Mia, and felt this Hawaiian had busted up his chances. Phillipo vowed he would have her one day.
  Babs walked over to them in the doorway. "You guys looking for Eva and Treb?" she didn't wait for an answer. "They're over there. What the hell happened to them? Someone sprinkle pixie dust on em? They haven't stopped smiling since they walked in."
  As they walked around the pool table Mia felt Dick's hand tighten on hers. It was obvious something had changed. They didn't look like brother and sister anymore.
  "What happened to you two?" Mia asked.
  "Yeah," Dick added. "You guys look like you fell in a vat of syrup. It's disgusting."
  Treb looked up at them standing there, "Now you know what we've been putting up with for the last few months. Now it's our turn."
  Eva's eyes were sparkling and at that moment Mia thought Eva had to be the prettiest and happiest

woman in the world.

"You guys can finish our drinks," Eva said, looking more at Mia and smiling," I have to take this guy up to the house for awhile. We have a lot of lost time to make up for, and he's not getting any younger."

Dick stood there with his mouth hanging open as the two of them walked out the door. "Now what the hell do you think happened to them in the last hour?"

.....

The walk back to the house was both an eternity and a fleeting moment for Treb. He was fighting a battle in his head. Guilt was telling him there was something wrong here. That he shouldn't be doing this. Then he would glance at Eva walking next to him, and he knew what they were doing was right.

On the way they stopped at a small gift store. The girl that worked there knew them and nodded to them as they walked in. Treb picked up a necklace. It was a fine gold chain with a gold plated shell hanging from it. It was one of the biggest selling tourist items on Catalina. He hung it on her neck and paid the girl at the counter. Once they were outside she pulled him to her saying, "I'll never take it off."

They walked to the house. Once inside they walked into the bedroom. Eva turned and looked into his eyes.

"I love you," was all she said, and she melted into his arms.

It was almost like a dream. They kissed for what seemed like an eternity. Slowly Treb lowered her to the bed. She lay there like a trusting child. Her deep blue/green eyes looking up at him with adoration and love. For a long time he lay beside her, running his fingers over her face and kissing her very softly.

She moaned and pulled him to her. His hands moved down her back, the warmth of her skin was like electricity. Her shorts fell to the floor and they were followed by her halter top. In a trance he watched as she sat above him on the bed, taking his T-shirt off. She sat astride him and softly rubbed his chest. Kissing each of his nipples. She slid farther down kissing her way down his hard stomach, undoing his Levi's as she went. A moment later her head was in his lap, taking his hard manhood into her mouth.

Slow and soft she moved her head up and down feeling the hardness. Four or five times he was near climax, and she would stop, moving up on him, kissing his stomach and chest, then moving down again.

He moved her around on the bed and picked her up as if she were a toy, bringing her legs around until they were in a 69 position. He used one of her legs as a pillow and started to nibble on the warm folds of her womanhood. All of a sudden he fell from her mouth and he heard her moan. At first softly, and then louder. She climaxed. It was long, and her whole body shuddered as she did.

He eased the way he held her but continued kissing her there. Soon she was moaning again, and once again she started to shudder, and climax.

She pushed him gently onto his back and took him into her mouth again, once again taking him to the edge. Then she got on top of him and guided him into her.

Looking up at her he thought she looked like an angel. She moved slowly at first, then increased the movement until she was about to cum again. This time she didn't pull away. She watched lovingly as his eyes closed and she felt him fill her as he reached the top.

They lay in each others arms exhausted. Finally she spoke in almost a whisper.

"That was the first time I ever made love," was all she said.

He understood.

17

The Land Rover bounced along a path that had been cut through the jungle by 50 generations of farmers. Driving was Jake Simms, in the passenger's seat, "Rabbit" Moriega. And in the backseat sat a man who didn't belong in Costa Rica. El Jeffe.

They were just north of La Cruz about 5 miles from the Nicaragua border. Once they were back in Nicaragua everything would be alright. El Jeffe's men would meet them there and take him back to Contra headquarters, across the border in Nicaragua.

The jungle was wet from rain and there was still a mist coming down.

Rabbit was speaking, "We're glad you made it back

alright. What do you figure happened?"

"Happened?" said El Jeffe, "I'll tell you what happened. Someone knew about the meeting and wanted to kill me and get their hands on the 110 kilos, that's what happened. What the fuck you think happened? What I want to know is who? It's your country. You better find out. That package is worth five million bucks and only I know where it is and how to bring it up. I want some answers and I want them soon. It's been months. We need those arms and ammunition now. I thought 'The Company' was supposed to have everything under control!"

Rabbit was burning inside, but he maintained his composure. "Yes sir. We know who set the bomb. It was that new man Tirantia had brought in. Al Huntington. Tirantia took care of him that night. No one has any idea of what went on. I was lucky those people stumbled on the boat and set off the explosion. Otherwise you would have been killed."

The Jeep bounced over a large hole filled with mud and it splashed over the Jeep, getting the men even dirtier than they were.

"Damnit Rabbit," Simms shouted, "would ya keep this fucking thing on the trail. Jesus H. Christ, I hate this God damned jungle!"

Simms wasn't pissed off about the jungle. Because of three stumble bum bikers he had lost half of a seven million dollar payoff. He couldn't figure out what went wrong. They had covered every possibility.

And now they had nothing. Back to square one. The miserable fucking jungle.

More mud splashed over them as they came upon the border. It was marked by a small plastic bag tided to a tree limb. As Rabbit pulled the Jeep to a stop, El Jeffe stood and got down from the back of the Jeep.

"I want Tirantia to have whatever help he needs to get the goods delivered," he said, "and we need the arms within one month. Understand?"

"Yeah," said Simms, "Yeah we understand. We'll handle it."

"Just don't handle it like last time," El Jeffe said, and turned back to walk to the waiting Jeep.

"Heffe," Simms shouted, "how will Tirantia be able to find the goods?"

He looked back at them. "When it's time, he will get what is needed.

As they turned the Jeep back towards the road to Puntarenas Jake Simms was in a terrible mood.

"Right now we were supposed to be sitting in Rio, sipping on a Pina Colada," he said. "Instead we're picking lice out of our fucking mud soaked shorts. Those fucking assholes had to fuck things up didn't they? Now how are we gonna get our hands on that shit and get it sold?"

Rabbit was used to him fuming. Ever since the explosion missed their intended target the man had been close to crazy.

"Hey," said Rabbit, "calm down will ya. We'll figure something out. All we had to do is find out where he hid the control device when he sank the boat, and where they dropped the drum. It had to be close to the West End. They didn't have time to go to sea before they scuttled the *Stone Witch*. Besides, you heard him say he'd tell Tirantia. As soon as he knows, we'll know.

"Do you think Tirantia has any idea where the stuff is?" asked Simms.

"No, I don't see how he could. He was on the other boat with the new guy when everything happened. He went back with Armando and didn't have a chance to see anything."

"Yeah," thought Simms out loud, "I guess you're right. How much farther to the paved road?"

Rabbit looked at his speedometer. "About ten more

miles. I sure will be glad to get back to Puntarenas and get some clean clothes on."

They rode in silence the rest of the way to the highway and kept going over things in their heads.

It had been a good plan and it should have worked. 110 kilos, over 240 pounds of pure Peruvian flake cocaine. After they stepped on it one time they would have over 480 pounds and get at least $15,000 a pound. Over $7,000,000 American dollars. Those stupid contras were losing over $2,000,000 by letting the CIA handle things for them.

But Rabbit Moriega and Jake Simms had very little to complain about with the CIA. They had both been with The Company for a long time. Simms since Vietnam and Rabbit since he left another "underground" government job. Both had managed to put away a comfortable little nest egg for retirement. This would have been the final score.

And it was safe, too. They had managed to convince Miles Kirkland, the Director of Covert Activities for the CIA that this was just a meeting, and that El Jeffe was getting too powerful. When they added a little info through an outside informer saying El Jeffe was stealing from the Contras that he led, it was all they needed. It should have gone simple and easy. No one else knew about that cocaine. They had kept that part quiet, just between Tirantia and themselves. Then the CIA would have moved Tirantia up into El Jeffe's place, and in a few months Rabbit and Simms could have retired in comfort. Everyone would have what they want.

They hit the paved section of road and turned south. The next 60 miles would go fast as they passed through nothing but miles and miles of jungle. Costa Rica was America's safe house in Central America and both men knew they had nothing to fear here. The only homes that could be seen from the road were small mud huts. The big Ranchos were off the road, behind private walls protected by private armies. They were owned by American corporations, and most of them were fronts for the CIA.

Rabbit had taken longer to turn against The Company than Simms did, but then he wasn't with them as long. He was a moralist. He had to believe in something to get involved. This had gotten him through Vietnam only because he stayed over there. If he had seen what was going on back at home he wouldn't have stayed. He believed he was doing something good for his country. When they came to him with a 'special' assignment he didn't even ask any questions. They took him out of Vietnam through a back door. A phony death. Then they set him up back home infiltrating the 'peaceniks'.

Once back in the Us he couldn't get used to the way people spoke against 'his' government. His first job was with a group called the Omega Squad. It was made up of undercover federal agents who would infiltrate outlaw motorcycle gangs and street gangs. Once they were in they would set them up so they could be taken down by the government. He stayed with them for almost two years, but he finally started to see what was really happening. He was so involved in what he was doing it almost passed him by that he was entrapping people. If he hadn't led them into doing these things, they probably wouldn't be doing them.

That was when he got involved with the Contras and the CIA. Finally he found a cause that seemed just. The United States had backed the Sandinistas in a takeover only to discover they were killing innocent people just like the Samosa Government they replaced. So the United States financed another coup to remove them.

Then the truth started to get through to Rabbit. He

had seen a lot of killing in his past, but nothing to compare with what the Contras were doing. Cold blooded murder was common. He was on one operation where Tirantia and fifty Contra soldiers, armed with guns and machetes wiped out a town of 250 people. Not just killed them, but wiped the town from the face of the earth. They beheaded children, raped and murdered the woman and tortured the men.

This particular operation was because one boy had stolen food from their camp. They found him in his village. They tied him up and made him watch as they took his seven year old sister and took turns raping and sodomizing her. Then they cut off her head. They did the same to his mother but they poured gasoline on her and torched her instead of beheading. He watched her die in flames. Then Tirantia had the boys hands cut off and so he would never steal again, using the flames of his burning mother to burn the wounds so he wouldn't bleed to death. The boy was the only one left alive in his village. This was so he could tell others what happened to people who stole from Tirantia.

And these were the people the United States were backing. These were the people Rabbit Moriega was supposed to be helping.

It was too much for him. All he wanted to do was get away, and that was when Jake Simms approached him with this plan.

And Tirantia, the man that led the raid, was their partner in this plan.

.....

The Rover pulled into Puntarenas and they parked in front of the hotel. It was small but clean. They walked into the bar. It was typical for the small coastal town. The rooms were on the second floor over the bar and restaurant. The bar itself had about as much atmosphere as a cafeteria. There were large windows in the front that were always left open, to allow some air in. Three of the four ceiling fans rotated slowly. The fourth hadn't worked in years. The walls were a off yellow. At one time they were probably white, but a million fly specks later they took on a yellowish tint.

The tables themselves were nothing more than tin-topped card tables with wooden legs nailed under them. Each proclaimed the name of a different brand of beer.

Rabbit walked to one that wasn't quite as filthy as the others and pulled a small wooden chair up. Simms did the same, banging on it to knock the flies off as he sat.

"Ok," Simms said," now let's figure out what we're going to do about this. Any ideas?"

Rabbit thought for a minute.

"Look we know the coke is somewhere off the West End of Catalina, right? And we know that the sender to activate the air bag is somewhere on the island. He had to leave it there when he swam ashore after the boat went down. The only thing we don't know is who else knows where the goods are. If the boat Captain or any of the crew know they could get to it first, and all this will be for nothing."

"So what next?" Simms asked, speaking more to himself then to Rabbit, "what's our next step?"

He stared off into space in front of him. They were both silent, then they looked at each other.

"Tirantia!" Rabbit said, and Simms smiled at him as if he knew what he was thinking. "What was Tirantia doing on the other boat with Armando and the new guy?" He didn't wait for an answer, "he was planning to take the shit himself! He was going to cut us out! He lets us do the dirty work and then goes for the goodies without us!"

"Right!" this time Simms was getting excited, "He wasn't suppose to be at the meeting. He was just supposed to set it up. El Jeffe was supposed to arrange for the transfer of the goods and arms with the new guy. Why was Tirantia there?"

They both sat for a long time in silence.

"We need to get El Jeffe to talk," said Simms. "The only question is how?"

18

A small blue inflatable boat started out of Isthmus Cove heading around towards Emerald Cove. Treb and Dick sat opposite each other in the rear of the boat while Eva and Mia sat near the bow. Between them were scuba tanks and diving gear.

"Have you got the grid map?" Treb asked.

"Yeah, right here."

Dick took a small chart out of his pocket and laid it across the equipment. It was a chart of Emerald Bay with a grid marked over it, marking it into sections of about twenty feet square. Where the boat exploded was marked on the chart as well as where the hull came to rest before it was hauled up and taken to a shipyard on the mainland.

All of the grids between where the boat exploded and where it landed were marked off with an initial showing who had searched that area.

"I was thinking today I might search the base of the reef," Treb said, pointing to a section on the far side, where the reef dropped off fast to a deep level.

Dick looked over the chart.

"Probably a good idea. This summer the shallows were pretty well picked over. If we are going to find anything we would have found it by now. He looked over the chart more carefully. "Look here, where the reef drops off fast. If something washed along here it could fall down that crevice and never be seen again."

Mia and Eva were busy smearing their bodies with suntan oil. They were used to the guys getting lost in their search. Eva wanted to find out who killed Karen almost as much as Treb did.

They landed the boat at the base of Indian Rock. The girls took their towels and laid them out where they could get plenty of sun. Meanwhile Treb and Dick started their ritual of getting ready to dive.

The water was warm enough so they didn't need wetsuits. They strapped their aluminum tanks onto their Buoyancy Compensators and checked each others regulators to make sure they were turned on. Then they put on their fins, masks, and snorkels. After they attached weight belts it was time to go in.

Treb rolled backwards into the water first. He checked the timer on his wrist and set it. Then he released some of the air from his BC until he started to sink slowly. He followed the anchor line down to the bottom, where it sat about eight feet down nestled into the reef. He moved the anchor around a little until it was well secured. He looked over at Dick and gave him the thumbs up.

They glided over the reef as if they were flying in slow motion. Above it was a warm and calm day which made the water even clearer than usual. The visibility was well over 100 feet. Excellent.

They made their way east across the reef, colorful fish ignoring them, occasionally watching with curiosity. Once they were around Indian Rock they headed a little north to where the reef dropped off into the canyon that joined with the San Pedro channel. At the end of the reef Dick pounded a small marker into the reef with his sampling hammer. A small orange dot. This way they could mark and chart where they had searched on the grid map when they returned.

Then they started down the face of the reef. They stayed about twenty feet apart and moved down slowly. They could search the little cracks and crevices as they descended. The reef dropped off at a steep angle and they searched carefully. As they went down they watched their depth gauges. The reef dropped off fast, and they had to watch their bottom time and depth to avoid Nitrogen Narcosis.

Nitrogen Narcosis, also known as the Bends, can sneak up on you fast. If you stay too deep too long the nitrogen in your system compresses faster than the other gases. If you come up fast it forms bubbles in your joints and as they decompress the joints are pried apart. It's painful as hell.

They knew this and watched their depth carefully.

At fifty feet they stopped and signaled to each other. They would search an area 40 feet across and work their way up. Each man let a little air in from their tank into the BC, and they started their slow ascent, searching every nook and cranny as they went up.

They searched for a little over a half hour and headed back to the boat for their second tanks. They would just make two dives today.

They took a little break between dives to allow their systems to "air out" some. They stretched out near the girls and discussed the grip map, marking where

151

they'd searched. The sun warmed them.

"Man, it sure is pretty down there, isn't it?" dick said.

"Sure is. Got kinda cold down at 50 feet though," Treb said. "Did you see that crack running down the face of the reef? Looked like it wasn't too old. I found a Pepsi bottle that was jammed into it and it was broken. Looked like the reef shifted and cut the bottle in half. Weird huh?"

"It wasn't where I was," said Dick," I'll check it out when we go down again. How deep do you want to go?"

Treb looked at his time and depth guide. "We shouldn't go deeper then 100 feet and no longer then 15 minutes at that depth, then we come up slow, at least 10 minutes to the top, ok?"

"Sounds good to me. It's gonna get cold at that depth. Ready to hit it?"

"Let's do it," Treb said, and he slapped Eva's butt playfully.

"Hey," she shouted, and then grabbed him. "Think you can beat me, huh?"

She pulled him down on top of her. He could feel the warmth of her skin covered with the oil, and all of a sudden wished they were somewhere alone.

"Okay, time for that later," Mia said, pulling Eva off Treb and laughing. "I go on duty in an hour and if you two get started we'll never get back to town."

They donned their gear again and in a few minutes were gliding over the reef again. Dick spotted the marker and waved to Treb, pointing to it. Once again they went over the side of the reef and headed down. This time faster. They would drop to the 100 foot depth and then work their way up slowly, allowing the pressure in the bodies to neutralize.

When they reached the 100 foot level Treb signaled to Dick and they stopped. Treb looked over and held up one finger, meaning to wait a minute. He swam away from the reef about thirty feet and turned around, looking back at the face of the reef. He was looking for the crack he'd found earlier.

All of a sudden he started to signal to Dick with both arms. At first Dick thought there might be a shark nearby, but he looked around and didn't see one, so he swam over to where Treb was floating and turned around to look at the reef.

About fifty feet below where they were the small crack that Treb was talking about earlier opened up. From there to bottom, about another 100 feet, it gradually opened until, at about 225 feet it looked like it was big enough for a man to go inside.

Treb signaled to Dick by pointing to himself and to the cave. Dick pointed to his watch, telling him to watch his time. Treb shook his head affirmative and headed down. It only took him a couple of minutes to get down, and then he looked inside. It was dark, real dark, and they hadn't brought any lights with them. He was about 230 feet down and only had a few more safe minutes. His eyes followed the crack toward the bottom a little below him. Something glinted and caught his eye. In the dim light, after it filtered down through 260 feet of water, something would have to be awfully reflective to glimmer.

Treb checked his timer and depth gauge. It would be cutting it close, but he had to check. It might be something that could lead him to the people who killed Karen and Rom.

As he approached the object he started to feel lightheaded. The first sign of The Bends. They used to call it Rapture of the Deep because you get almost giddy before you lose it completely.

He reached down and grabbed the glinting object, staring at it like a small boy who would look at an insect in his hand. He was losing it. He felt giddy and as if he could stay down there forever.

All of a sudden he felt himself pulled up by his tank. Dick was watching him and saw his dreamlike movements. He guessed what was happening.

They went up slowly. Stopping every twenty feet for a couple of minutes. By the time they reached the top Treb was feeling normal again.

They started back to the boat and climbed in, taking off their equipment.

"What was it?" Dick asked.

"I don't know. Some kind of coin. Looks like silver or something, but it's real shiny, like it's new. Probably a silver dollar," and he reached into the pocket of his bathing suit.

When he took it out his mouth hung open. He handed it to Dick and his did the same.

The blue of the water at 260 feet filters out the red light like a filter, making the color disappear.

What Treb thought was a silver quarter was actually a very old gold coin.

"It looks like gold!" they both said.

The trip back to the Isthmus was very quiet. The four of them were all deep in thought. A gold coin at the bottom of the ocean is quite a find, and they all knew that, but there was more to it than that. The coin was clean. It wasn't covered with coral or other sea growth. How did it stay like that? Was it just dropped? And how old was it?

When they reached the Isthmus they showered and dressed. Mia had to be on the job in less than an hour and the drive to Avalon was a tedious one. By the time they reached town they were all dreamed out. Treasures of the deep buried by pirates seemed almost ludicrous.

They dropped Eva and Mia off at the house so Mia could get ready for work and headed over to the sheriff's office. They decided to show him the coin

Emerald Bay

and see what he thought. He'd been around a lot of years and was pretty savvy about the history of Catalina. It was kind of a hobby with him.

When they reached his office they handed him the coin. He studied it careful and took out a small magnifying glass.

"Where was this when you found it?" he asked Treb.

Treb thought for a minute. Should he tell him? Could he be trusted? Then he realized he could probably trust this man more than anyone else alive.

"At the base of the reef over by Indian Rock in Emerald Bay. Do you know the place?"

Sheriff Bob sat back and put his feet up on his desk in his 'thinking' position. Then he reached behind him for a book. It was The History of the Channel Islands.

Mia walked in and poured them all some coffee.

"Well Bob," she said, handing him his favorite cup filled with coffee and extra cream, the way he liked it, "whadaya think? Are we rich, or what?"

He was busy flipping through the pages of the book and didn't look up. "You might be, you just might be," and he kept reading.

Finally he looked up from the book and looked over his glasses at Treb.

"There are four possibilities,"; he said, looking very serious. "One ship went down in 1598 with a lot of bullion, but I don't think this is from that wreck. They found most of that in the late 1890's and besides that, it wasn't coin." He thought some more.

"No," he thought further. "Couldn't have been that one. That was off Ship Rock and the current runs the other way."

He looked at the book some more, and then studied the coin again.

"It's possible that this has something to do with the Spanish Frigate that went down in 1852. Most of its value was in cargo. Lots of gold and jewelry was reported to be lost. Never was recovered."

He looked at the coin a little longer.

"You said four possibilities," Treb asked," what are the others?"

"An even longer shot then the Frigate in 1852. In the early eighteen hundreds, around the turn of the century, there was a pirate named Hypolite Blanchard. His ship was pretty badly beaten trying to take some booty on Santa Cruz Island. They say he stopped in Emerald Bay for a few days to take on water and fresh meat. He was supposed to have a small amount of gold on board that he'd taken off a ship heading into San Francisco." The sheriff shrugged his shoulders, "they found a couple of graves over there from that period."

"The fourth possibility is probably what really happened though," he went on.

"What's that?" they all said, almost in unison.

"Someone had this coin as a lucky piece and it fell out of their pocket while they were sailing by." He threw it to Treb. "God only knows."

Treb looked close at the coin, and took the magnifying glass off the desk.

"Could you make out any of the writing on the back?" he asked the older man.

"Nope. Just a face on the front and something odd on the back. It's pretty worn. That was probably the side it's been sitting on all these years."

"Wait a minute," Treb said. "Check it out closer. Look at the man's eyes!"

The sheriff took the coin back and the magnifying glass.

"I don't see anything strange," he said.

Dick took the coin and the glass. He studied the coin closely.

"By God. The motherfucker's Chinese!"

19

Eva finished washing the load of clothes in the washer and was putting them into the dryer. She was glad to have something to do to keep her busy, and she liked being able to help out. Mia had taken her in and she felt guilty about not helping with the rent. She'd gotten a job as a maid at one of the condos up the hill, but Mia wouldn't let her go her first day. She didn't want Eva cleaning up after people.

Mia had been talking to some of the shops in town, and there were a couple that were ready to start training her as a sales clerk. Eva liked that.

She thought about how her life had changed in the past few months. It was like a fairy tale.

Her friendship with Mia had grown to where the girls knew each other intimately. Late at night they would just sit and tell each other about their lives. She felt like she belonged. In Eva's letters to her mother she told her all about Mia and Dick, and she wrote the most about Treb. She had never met anyone like him.

At first, after the explosion, she'd felt guilty about his loss of Karen. She also felt guilty thinking the thoughts she had. He was so good to her, but he never asked anything in return. Not like all the other men she had known.

Even after they had been friends for months, the two of them could walk the beaches of Catalina at night, giving Mia and Dick some time alone. He would just talk.

She wanted to hear about Karen. She wanted to know every intimate detail of her life. It was their meeting that changed her whole life.

At first she was surprised. She found it hard to believe that the girl she met was once a hooker. The story about how Treb had met her, when she worked in a massage parlor for a motorcycle club made her feel strange. Then, after it sunk in, she realized she had even more respect for Treb after she knew. It took some kind of man to not only accept a woman after that, but to love her completely as he did.

It was while they sat out on those nights, talking, that she realized she knew what love was for the first time in her life. She sat and listened to Treb talk about his deepest inner feelings, and as she did, she fell in love with him.

It wasn't what she expected. There was no fire or burning to have physical contact with him. Just a warm feeling when they would walk together. A feeling that warmed her and surrounded her whenever they would be together. She loved watching him do little things like eat, or talk to Dick. She liked being with him. She was proud as he built himself up from an invalid, and she hurt with him when he would talk about his failures.

   Then there was the night they first held each other. She didn't know why she felt awkward with him until that night. They knew each other well, but there was one thing they never talked about. They had never spoken about the two of them together. It was almost like there was a guilt that stopped them. As if Karen's ghost kept them apart.

   The night they first embraced killed the ghosts. They both loved Karen, in different ways, but she was dead and they were still alive. A few weeks later Treb put it the best way she could imagine. If Karen could speak to them, she would want them to be together. They were both close to her.

   Her life changed completely. Suddenly there was a future to think about; plans to be made; things to look forward to. No longer was she just going through the action of living. No longer was her every thought about her mother. All of a sudden she found she felt good about herself. About her life and about her friends. She never thought life could be as good as this.

   The phone rang and she went into the kitchen to answer it.

   "Hi, Eva? This is Phillipo from down at the bar, is Mia there?"

   Eva didn't like the small man from the Twin Palms. He reminded her of the people that used to hang around with Al. She felt dirty whenever he looked at her.

   "No," she answered him, "she's at work. What do you want?"

   "Nothing, just wanted to know if she was there." He paused for a minute, "so you're there alone?"

   "Yes, why?" and before she finished he was off the

phone.

She walked back to the laundry room wondering what that had been all about and then soon forgot all about it. She had more pleasant things to think about, like the roast she was going to make for dinner tonight.

A knock on the door interrupted her thoughts.

"Just a minute," she said, stacking the folded clothes, and she walked to the door.

When she opened the door two men forced their way in. One looked like a football player. He wasn't smiling. Before she could move he was behind her while the other man put something over her nose and mouth. She could see Phillipo grinning from the side door of the van parked outside the door. Everything went black.

20

After Treb and Dick left the Sheriff's office they walked over to the Twin Palms. As they walked in Babs nodded to them. They waved to her and walked back to their booth at the rear of the place, near the pool table. They liked it there because it was dark.

Babs walked over and sat down next to Dick. She snuggled up to him playfully. "Hey, tall, dark, and ornamental, feel like a little Hiney?"

He knew she didn't mean Heineken beer by her tone, and laughed. He liked her sense of humor.

"No, sweetstuff, just a couple of Coor's."

As she got up to walk away he called after her. "Hey Babs, those shorts are sure tight. How do you get in em?"

"Well," she smiled," we could start with a couple of drinks." She chuckled as she walked over to the bar. Babs was Mia's friend and they all knew she kidded around with Dick.

Back at the table Treb and Dick hunched over and looked at their find.

"So what do ya think," Treb asked. "Is this somebody's lucky piece or have we found the treasure of the *Lost Dutchman*?

"Maybe the *Lost Chinaman*. This is definitely not Dutch," he responded.

They sat there looking at there find when Treb heard Babs from across the room.

"Hey big guy, telephone. You can get it over here."

He walked across to the bar and picked up the receiver. "This is Treb, go ahead."

Dick watched Treb's face turn red as he listened to the phone. It was pretty damned obvious something bad was wrong. He got up and walked over to where Treb was standing. Just as he got to the bar Treb hung up the phone and looked at him. He just stood there for a minute.

"Treb!" Dick reached out and put his hand on the big man's shoulder. "Treb, what is it?"

Treb started to come out of his trance.

"That was Sheriff Fox. He just talked to Danny, you know, Mia's next door neighbor? He saw two men taking Eva out of the house a few minutes ago."

"What do ya mean they were 'taking' her out of the house? Were they friends or what?" Dick asked.

"Doesn't sound like it. Let's get over there. Mia and Bob are going to meet us there."

Mia got to the house first. She'd pretty well looked it over by the time Treb and Dick arrived. When they came in she could see Treb wasn't going to like what they found.

"What happened?" he asked her.

"Well, it looks like a couple of guys just came in and grabbed her. There's no sign of a struggle. Nothing knocked over or broken. She's just gone."

She expected him to fly apart, but instead he just walked over to the kitchen counter and leaned back against it.

"Dick," Mia said, "would you go next door and get Danny? Let's see exactly what happened."

Just as Dick walked out the side door, Sheriff Fox came in the front.

He asked Mia if she had found anything.

"No, Sheriff. Nothing. No struggle. No fight and no blood. She's just gone."

Fox thought for a minute.

"Go through her stuff and see what's missing. Also see if what she was wearing is still here, or if she has changed."

"Ok boss," and she walked back towards the service porch where the clothes from the washer were stacked.

Sheriff Fox stood by the front door looking at the floor.

"Treb," he said. "Come over here a minute. Tell me if you smell something funny over here by the door."

Treb walked over. He did notice a strange odor.

"Yeah. It kinda smells like a hospital. Any idea what it is?"

Before he could say anything Dick returned with Danny, the man who saw Eva taken.

Treb walked over to the man, but Fox stopped him.

"Treb, go sit down in the other room. Let me take care of this. It's my job."

Treb walked back across the room, but didn't leave.

"Tell me exactly what you saw," Fox said to the man.

Danny was a small man. He'd lived next door to Mia as long as she'd lived there. They never spoke and she never saw him have any guests. He was one of those people that just exist without being seen.

"These two guys came to the door. I was just watering my Creeping Charlie's in the window," he pointed to some plants in a basket that hung at the top of his front window, "I saw that real pretty girl who lives here open the door, and they pushed their way in."

"What happened after that?" Fox asked him.

"I couldn't see inside the door, but in a couple of seconds they brought her out and put her into one of those Volkswagen vans. It looked like one of Ruby's Taxis."

"Can you describe the men?"

"Yeah. The big one looked like a football player. He had real big shoulders and a nice ass." Any questions about his being gay had just been answered.

"The other one wasn't as big, but he was very well built. He was Mexican or something. Dark hair, brown eyes, and a very dark complexion."

Fox looked at Mia. "Call Ruby and see if she knows anything." He turned back to Danny.

"Ok, come on in here and sit down. I want a complete description," and he led the man into the living room.

"Oh, one more thing," Danny said. "It looked like Phillipo was waiting in the van."

Treb and Dick stood there looking at each other.

"Phillipo?" Treb said. "What's he got to do with this?"

"I don't know," said Dick, 'but we're sure as hell going to find out."

"Dick," Treb asked, "did Eva ever talk to you about the guy she used to be with that disappeared? I think his name was Huntington?"

"A little. Not much though. Why?"

"There was something about a guy that looked like a football player. She laughed about it because the guy

Emerald Bay

was the first one who seemed to put Huntington in his place. He was a bodyguard or something."

Mia returned from the bedroom where she had used the phone to call Ruby's Cabs.

"Sounds like we're onto something. Two guys gave one of Ruby's drivers $300 to use a cab for thirty minutes. She hit the roof when she found out. She's going to bring the driver over to the sheriff's office in a couple of minutes."

"Just a minute," Treb said to Mia, "did Eva ever talk to you about some guy that looked like a football player?"

Mia thought,"Yeah, some guy that really put down old Greaseball." Then she looked at Treb and asked, "Why?"

"Danny says one of these dudes looked like a football player."

"Let's get down to the office and see what we can find out," Mia said.

"Yeah, but first let's try and find Phillipo," Treb and Dick said in unison.

After stopping at his apartment and calling the Twin Palms, they went to the Sheriff's office. Ruby and her driver had left the office, and the Sheriff, Mia, Dick, and Treb sat around comparing notes.

"Ok," started the Sheriff, "let's see what we have. Two guys come in and snatch Eva." Treb winced a little at the cold way it was stated, but the Sheriff went on. "Looks like they used ether to knock her out and keep her quiet. One of the guys sounds like someone from her past. We know they used one of Ruby's cabs and they left the cab in the lot over by Descanso Beach. That would indicate a boat was used to get her off the island. Everyone agree so far?"

"Don't forget Phillipo." Treb interjected.

Everyone was silent.

"Ok, now let's see if we can figure out what's behind

all this."

"Mia," it was Treb talking. "Did Eva ever tell you about the big house in Beverly Hills they went to just before they came over to Emerald Bay?"

"Yeah," she said," it was some friend of... wait a minute! That was where she saw the guy that looked like a football player!"

"Do you remember the guy's name?"

"One of the guys was Armando, I think the one that owned the house. The other one had a weird name. A nickname, Tigre, that was it."

Treb stood up.

"Dick, let's get outta here. We aren't getting a fucking thing done here."

"Yeah, fuck this sitting around." Treb said, and with that they were out of the door.

Sheriff Fox watched as they left. "Damned hotheads."

He picked up the phone as he opened his tattered leather phone book. He searched for a minute and dialed a ten digit number in Washington DC. Mia just sat there and watched him.

"Are you sure the name was Tigre?" he asked her, and before she could answer he spoke into the phone.

"AGC 309," he said into the receiver, then he waited a minute. "Fox, AGC 309. Kirkland, DCA 269... I'll wait."

In a minute someone came on the other end of the line.

"Miles, you old con man, this is Fox. Long time."

21

The plane from Catalina Island landed in Long Beach at 5:30 p.m. As soon as it touched down Treb and Dick headed to the phone booth inside the terminal. Treb dialed a number and waited.

"Matt," he said into the phone, "this is Treb. I've got some trouble. Can you pick me and Dick up at the Long Beach airport?" He waited a second and then continued, "Yeah I know. What time is the meeting tonight?" He waited again. "Ok, we'll see you outside the terminal in a little bit. Thanks."

He hung up the phone and dialed another number.

"Country, this is Treb. I've got a problem and I'd like to ask the club for help. Is it okay if Dick and I come to the meeting tonight?"

A few minutes later Treb and Dick were met in front of the terminal by a stretch limo, the same one Treb had ridden in on his wedding day. The limo service was owned by Franko, one of the club members. He'd loaned it to Matt to pick up the two retired members.

On the way to the clubhouse he and Dick explained what had happened. Soon they arrived at the clubhouse.

The Warriors clubhouse was an old bar the club had bought years ago and turned into a clubhouse and party place. As they parked the car Treb looked at the old building and a bunch of memories started to come back. For a lot of years this place had been his home away form home. Returning felt just as is he were coming home.

The *Warrior Room*, as it was called, sat where three streets intersected, making a small wedge shaped block. That was the corner the clubhouse sat on. The parking lot was the very corner, and it was filled with Harleys. The bar set back a little with some trees around it.

As they entered the bar area Treb and Dick were surrounded by the members. The Warriors was an old club, and most of the members had been riding bikes for years. Many of them were what they call "Grey Beards;" older members who'd been riding for 20 years or more, but there was a vitality in the room that couldn't be denied. There was also a deep trust. There had been no new members in years, and those who were still active in the club had known and counted on each other for a long time.

Everyone was talking at once, and soon Treb and Dick found themselves with cold beer and surrounded by old friends. The meeting was scheduled for eight o'clock, in about twenty minutes, so they all had time to talk over the old days.

At the appointed time all of the old ladies stayed out in the bar, while the members went back into what was once the owner's apartment at the rear of the bar. After everyone sat down, Country, the president, called the meeting to order.

As was the custom, before anything was said at the meeting the two retired members were introduced and the membership was asked if anyone had anything to say against them being in the room during the meeting. If there had been one patcholder who didn't like it, they would have to leave. No one objected.

After roll call was over and the meeting was starting Treb raised his hand and asked to be recognized.

He started to tell them what was going on. He filled them in on what had happened and finished with," I need some help. My ol lady has been kidnapped and I am going to try and get her back. I don't know why she was taken, but the people who did it are pretty well connected."

Clean Cut, one of the old time members, raised his hand to ask a question.

"Yeah Cut?"

"Look Bro, you may be retired, but yer still one of us. What's the deal?"

The rest of the members murmured their agreement.

"Ok," he smiled, "and thanks."

"Fuck you," smiled Clean Cut, and they had to wait for the noise to die down in the room.

"There's some dude named 'Armando' up in Beverly Hills. He's moving a bunch of coke. First, I need to find out where his place is, and then see if that's where Eva is."

The club knew what had happened to Karen, they'd all loved her like a sister. They also knew about Treb's new girl. It obviously meant a lot to him.

Franko spoke up from the far side of the room.

"I know the dude. I used to score some shit from him until the Chinks beat his price." Everyone laughed. Frank went on, "He still uses my limo's some time. How much time we got to check this shit out?"

Treb just looked down.

Then Dick broke in. "They snatched her this afternoon. We don't know why, but we do know these assholes are dangerous. We need info fast."

"Look guys," Treb said," I don't want the club getting into any shit over this. Dick and I can handle getting her back. We just need to know where she is. Ok?"

Franko smiled.

"What the fuck Bro, why didn't you just call?" and he threw Treb a piece of paper from across the room. It was wrapped around a 2 gram vile of coke. It was full. There was an address in Truesdale Estates written on the paper.

"Now," continued Franko, smiling, "you wanna get the fuck out so we can finish this bullshit meeting and get into party mode?"

The whole room was laughing as Treb and Dick went outside to the bar and had a few more brews.

After the meeting was over Franko came over to where the two of them were sitting.

"Before you guys go up there playing Kung Fu, I think we'd better sit down and do some talking. It ain't gonna be easy getting in there, and it'll be even harder getting out."

Since the meeting was over most of the members had come back out to the bar. There were five or six members still in the back room, which was off limits to the ol' ladies. A poker game was in full swing. Franko walked them back to one of the sofas that surrounded the room and they sat down.

"Look Brothers," he started, "all kidding aside. This

asshole is right up there on top. No bullshit games, you dig?"

Treb and Dick just shook their heads.

"Now, I've been up there a couple of times when he had his 'special' people and didn't want just any driver, if you know what I mean. The place is bugged to the hilt. Armed guards, video surveillance, dogs, you know the drill. The whole fucking nine yards," Franko looked at the two of them and knew they were going anyway.

"Give me a couple of minutes and I'll give you a kind of layout. Meanwhile I'd go see Bobby," Franko was referring to one of the members that was heavy into weapons, "you're gonna need some shit. I'll be out in a few minutes with the sketch."

In the bar out front they found Bobby behind the bar serving up the beer. They talked with him for awhile and before they finished Franko walked over. He spread a piece of paper out on the bar. The four of them looked at it.

After Frank explained where the cameras were and where the guards he knew about were normally stationed, Bobby broke in.

"You're gonna need some firepower. Short range and not much re-loading time. You mind if I come along? This sounds like fun."

Treb looked at Dick, then over at Bobby.

"Look Brother, this could be pretty heavy," Treb said. "I don't want the club getting fucked up over my shit."

Bobby put his hand on Treb's arm.

"Treb, I left Nam in 1968. It was the best home I ever knew next to this place," he indicated the clubhouse, "Over twenty years since I've had any real fun. This ain't the club talking. It's me. Bobby. A friend. A brother. I want in, ok?"

Treb smiled at him.

"Ok, Brother, if it's just for fun, let's do it."

Franko broke in. "You guys gonna waste this Armando dude?"

Treb thought of why they'd taken Eva, and that they were most likely responsible for Rom and Karen's death. "Yeah, why not?"

Franko broke into a big grin. "then I might as well go. Won't matter if he sees me or not. He won't be able to tell no one, ain't it? Who says we're too old to have fun?"

22

Sheriff Fox and Mia sat at a back booth in The Galleon. It was Bob's favorite restaurant on the Island. The waitress poured some wine out of the decanter into the two cut crystal glasses and asked if they needed anything else.

"No thanks, Penny. We'll order in a minute." Bob said, "Thanks," then he turned back to Mia.

"Look, Mia, I know you're confused and worried. That's why I brought you here, maybe I can straighten some of this out for you. Ok?"

"Yeah, but how..?"

"Just relax and I'll tell you what I know. Here, have some more wine," and he poured her glass full again.

Bob took a long drink of the deep red wine from his glass and sat back.

"The man I was talking to back at the office was Miles Kirkland. He's the Director of Covert Activities for the good guys," he smiled, "that means us."

"I know I never talked much about my past, but he and I were partners back when I was in the CIA. By the way, you never really leave the CIA, you just kind of go inactive. That's what I did." He took another sip and went on.

"After we helped the Sandinistas overthrow the Samosa Government in Nicaragua I'd had enough. 35 years was enough to give to my country, so I just took this job and kicked back. Miles was younger than me, and he stayed active. A couple years ago they made him DCO. He's a good man."

Mia asked, "What's that all got to do with what' going on here?"

She thought maybe he was so befuddled by what went on he was losing touch with reality. He could hear it in her voice. She soon found that she was underestimating the man.

"Tigre was the clue I needed. His real name is Jose Tirantia. He was the number two man with the Contras." He saw a look of confusion in her face, so he explained.

"The Contras were the people in Nicaragua that were trying to overthrow the Sandinistas. Understand?"

"Yeah, but you said you helped the Sandinistas, so that must mean the Contras are the bad guys. What was he doing here in the United States?" She still looked confused.

"Well, it turned out that the Sandinistas were just as bad as the Samosa Regime, so we we're helping to overthrow them too. Get it?"

"Not really," she sat back and took another sip from

the glass, "but go on. What's all this got to do with Eva?"

Bob signaled for Penny to fill the wine decanter again, and he continued.

"We're not sure where Eva fits into this, but if what Miles tells me can be confirmed, the explosion that killed Karen and Rom was set by the CIA."

Mia dropped her glass on the table and fell back onto her chair.

"The CIA? What the hell are they doing planting bombs here in the United States? I thought they were only supposed to screw up other people's countries!"

All of a sudden the futility of the two people's deaths seemed to hit her. The frustration turned to anger. People at the other tables just stared as she raved.

"Mia," Fox was saying, "keep it down. This isn't for the news media, understand?"

Just then Penny came back over to the table.

"Sheriff," she said, "there's a phone call for you up at the counter."

He got up and excused himself, walking to the counter.

In a minute he was back.

"Captain Kirk down at Catalina Express just called in. Phillipo was trying to take the shuttle back to the mainland. I'm going across the street for a second to talk to him. I'll be right back."

"I'll go with you," she said.

He put his hand on her shoulder gently holding her in her seat.

"No honey, I don't have time to play nice sheriff. I'm going to get some answers and I don't want you involved. Just tell Penny to keep things warm and I'll be back in five minutes."

Exactly five minutes later he walked back into the door.

"It was the guy that worked for Armando.' He said. "They took her to his place."

She noticed he was holding his right hand and that there were bruises on it.

"How did he get involved, and how did you know he would know where they took her?" She looked amazed.

"Mia," he said, "Phillipo has been handling the coke and grass here for a couple of years. I knew it, but there was so little going on I just kept an eye on him. His connection was Armando. They've been watching him for some time."

"Who's 'they'?" she asked almost dumfounded. She couldn't believe he knew all this and she didn't have a clue.

"The company," was all he said. Then he reached for his glass and filled it.

She slowly shook her head and sat forward. He filled her glass and she downed it in one swallow. The alcohol was starting to warm her.

"There's more," Fox went on. "This all has something to do with trading cocaine to the United States for Arms for the Contras. It seems that in their infinite wisdom the government figures they could take the drugs and destroy them, keeping them off the streets, and get a little something for the arms that they would normally give the Contras."

"Doesn't that force the Contras to become drug smugglers?" she looked even more confused, "Why would the US do that?"

Fox smiled and took another drink.

"Now you're starting to understand why I left The Company."

Mia shook her head a little. The wine was starting to get to her. That was what Bob had wanted. The less she remembered about what he said the better. He had been careful for too many years to let this out, but he loved her like a daughter, and he had to try and help her.

"I still can't see how Eva's messed up in this. Why would they want her?" she said looking even more dazed than she did a minute ago. Fox waved to Penny and she brought another decanter to the table, smiling.

"And," she continued, "what's going to happen to Treb and Dick. Their out there, God only knows where, trying to find her. They could get killed!"

"I wouldn't worry too much about them. Treb can take care of himself and Dick's been through plenty of action." He took another drink.

Mia stared at him for a minute. Her eyes were a little blurry.

"What'ya mean been through a lot?" She was starting to slur her words. "What'daya know about Dick?"

He sat forward in his chair and looked at her for a minute. Then he reached over and took the glass out of her hand and set it down.

"Mia, as soon as you started seeing Dick I ran a check on him."

"You did what?" she asked in a loud voice. "What gave you the right?"

"I love you. That's what gave me the right. Do you understand that?"

She looked at him and instantly calmed down. She put her hand on his on top of the table.

"Yeah," she said. "I understand. I love you too, you old fart."

"Anyway," he continued, trying not to get too maudlin, "did you know that he was an honest to goodness hero in Vietnam?"

Mia shook her head. "No, I knew he was there, but he doesn't talk about it much."

"Well he should. In his tour over there he was

decorated more than a Christmas tree. A bunch of purple hearts, Distinguished Service Cross, and he was even nominated for the Congressional Medal of Honor."

"Nominated," she asked, "did he get it?"

"No. there was something about him killing the man who nominated him. His superior officer. Must not have been out of whack because he was never charged and when he returned he got an Honorable Discharge. I'm not sure of the whole thing. I just did a preliminary to make sure you weren't seeing an axe murderer.

"Ok," she smiled at him, proud of what she had just found out. "So he's not an axe murderer, what did you find out about Treb?"

"Pretty interesting. Until I got to know him I was worried about you hanging around with him. He did his time in Vietnam, but nothing special. After he got out he started riding a motorcycle. He was in a club, and raised a lot of hell. Then a few years ago he led the bikers in a fight against a federal helmet law being enacted. The government got a little worried because he united all the outlaw clubs, and they had been trying to keep the clubs at war with each other. It was a national protest and the shit hit the fan. They came after him pretty hard."

"Is that it?" she asked.

"Almost." He went on. "They had him for killing a cop, but it turned out to be an undercover man who wasn't in uniform and was shooting at him. Self defense. He was cleared. That was about it. After that , nothing."

Penny had brought over two cups of coffee. Mia picked hers up and took a sip, wincing as the hot liquid burned her lip.

"But with all this we don't know why they took Eva?" she asked, licking the burn.

"No," he shook his head. "There doesn't seem to be an real connection between Tirantia and her." He took a sip of coffee," but Miles is still working on it."

Bob Bitchin

23

Franko's limo pulled up about a block from Armando's and parked away from the streetlights. Treb, Dick, and Bobby joined him near the truck and they went over things one last time. It was ten minutes until midnight.

Getting into the yard wouldn't be too bad. The wall was low enough and had enough trees around to make it pretty easy. They knew where most of the cameras were, and how to avoid them. That just left the dogs. There were two of them. Both Rottweilers and both well trained. This is where Bobby's expertise came in. He'd worked with K-9's in Nam.

There were three entrances to the house. The front

and rear doors, and a patio entrance near the pool. Since Franko didn't know the interior layout they weren't sure which of these would be best, so they decided to just play it as they went.

They divided into two teams. Treb and Dick went around the right side of the wall, Bobby and Franko went left. Treb and Dick found a tree that looked pretty easy to get over and climbed to the top of the wall. They searched the grounds for the cameras that Franko had told them about, and found one other. They checked their watches. One more minute and it would be midnight. Treb's eyes searched the windows for some sign of Eva, but saw none.

There was a long black Mercedes parked near the rear entrance and one man was leaning against it. Another guard was on an upper floor balcony. He was sitting on a chair smoking a cigarette. It was obvious they weren't expecting anything unusual.

At precisely midnight they dropped over the wall and made their way behind the shrubs to stay out of the cameras view. Treb held a Mac 10 with a silencer and flame suppressor and had a Walther PPK .9 millimeter automatic tucked in his belt. Dick had an automatic crossbow like the one he'd used when he was in Nam. It had four arrows pre set so all he had to do was restring and the next arrow was ready to go. He also had a Colt Military .45 automatic.

They headed towards the back of the house. When they were about 30 yards from the man by the Mercedes Dick touched Treb's arm signaling him to stop. He put the bow up to a firing position and let on fly. The whistle of the shaft in flight sounded loud to them, but the man never heard it. When it hit his head he just toppled over backwards.

All of a sudden they heard a dog running through the brush. As the dog let out its first yelp Treb pulled one of the special gas canisters that Bobby had given him from his belt, and lobbed it halfway between him and the dog. As the dog hit the blue haze he tried to keep running, but slowly sank to his knees, and then fell over on his side. His tongue lolling out of his mouth. He would be out for hours.

They heard barking from the other side of the house and knew it had to be Bobby and Franko. It stopped almost as fast as it started, but too late. The guard on the balcony had his gun out and was staring at the other side.

Before Treb could think Dick had gotten behind the nearest camera and was at the side of the house. He jumped up and reached the bottom of the balcony, pulling himself up in one move. Before the man could even turn around Dick slammed the base of his skull with the bow. He then lowered the man's body to the deck, his neck broken. He turned and signaled to Treb.

Two men appeared through the rear door near the car. Treb raised the Mac and started shooting. Even with the silencer the shots shattered the quiet of the night. Both men were dead before they were on the ground.

Now they heard shooting from the other side of the house. Dick signaled for Treb to go in through the back door as he entered the house through the balcony.

Once inside the door Treb got a little confused. There were two hallways. One went left into the kitchen, the other looked like it went into a maid's quarters or something. He turned left and tucked close into the wall, using the doorways for cover. He worked his way farther into the house. All of a sudden there was a shot from behind him. It hit his side and he spun and went down, firing the Mac 10 as he turned . He saw the man fall.

He got up and his side was bleeding. He could feel

the warmth of his blood as it ran down his side. Then there was another man in front of him. He fired with the Mac until it stopped firing, empty. The man was hit at least eight times, and dead by the time the fourth or fifth bullet hit.

Treb stepped over the body and made his way into the dining room.

Upstairs Dick had found the room where two guards were monitoring the cameras. He walked into the room and they were both on the floor in a matter of seconds. A third man came in from a side door and he hit him with a swing kick that could have put a horse out. Then he started the search. He went to each door on the floor and kicked it open, one by one he checked each room. As he reached the end of the hallway he heard a sound behind him and spun around with his pistol out. It was Bobby. He'd come up the south stairway. Together they started to clear the floor just as if they were back in Vietnam. No fear, just an adrenaline rush that bordered on a high. They worked their way down the hallway, until they were outside the double doors of the office. The man had to be here. They looked at each other and Dick gave Bobby the signal to take him alive if possible.

The door gave with the first kick. They both stepped back outside the room as bullets filled the air and slammed into the opposite wall. They waited for a two-count, and then they jumped into the room, crossing each others paths and rolling on the floor in two directions. Armando and the football player opened up with a pair of Uzi 9 mm machine pistols. The walls were turned to paper maché but Dick and Bobby were too fast. They rolled across the floor and Dick came up under the football players jaw with a kick from his laying position. Bobby tackled Armando and the man went down,. losing control of the Uzi and spraying the ceiling.

When Treb came through the door he found Dick standing over the football player, the big man out cold, and Bobby had Armando in his chair behind his desk, with a Buckmaster survival knife snug under his chin.

"All right asshole, where's the girl?" he was asking.

Just then Treb spun around. He heard the sound of tires speeding away from the back door.

"Jesus Fucking Christ, I forgot the maid's rooms," and he ran towards the back of the house. As he got outside the back door he could see the taillights of the Mercedes speeding out onto Hillside Drive.

He was holding his side as he walked back into the office, and his eyes were blazing. He walked over to where Armando was sitting.

"Ok, greaseball," he said, pulling the man's hair and jerking his head back against the chair, "where the fuck are they going?"

Armando just looked at him and smiled.

Bobby looked at Treb and said "Hey bro, let me handle this. I hate to think my military training went for nothing."

Bobby took his knife and held it against the base of Armando's little finger.

"The girl, where?"

Armando looked scared. "Yo-you wouldn't. That-I don't - what girl?"

"Wrong answer," said Bobby, and the finger dropped onto the desk.

For a full second Armando jus stared at his finger laying on the desk. Then he started screaming. "you can't do this. Do you know who I am? I'm gonna bleed to death! You fucking punks!"

Bobby just looked down at him. He was still smiling. He hooked the knife under the man's thumb on his opposite hand.

"The girl. Where?"

"Tigre- it was Tigre. He wanted her for something.

I don't know-he never said. Just said he needed her. I swear. I swear"

Bobby smiled and pulled the knife a little tighter.

"Good. Good. Now you know how to play. Let's get on with the fun. Who blew up the boat in Emerald Bay last year?"

Once again Armando looked confused, but they could see shock was starting to set in. his face was white and a cold sweat had broken out. "I didn't know anything about it.-it was Tigre- said it had something to do with a big shipment. He wouldn't tell me."

As he spoke his foot was searching the floor. Under the desk was the button that controlled an electrically operated machine gun mounted in an alcove behind the mirror across from his desk. As his foot his the button he ducked to get below the desk, which was the pre-set line of fire. Bobby and Dick both saw something in his eyes, and as he started to duck they guessed something was wrong. Dick hit Treb with a body block and they fell to the floor. Bobby rolled to the floor and pushed Armando's body back into the chair, right into the line of fire. It almost cut him in half.

They walked back out to the entryway and found Franko still sitting there with two guards.

"These guys don't know anything. Just hired," he said, "what do ya wanna do with em?"

There was terror in both men's eyes.

Dick looked at the bigger of the two, then he stuck his bow under the man's chin, holding the razor sharp arrow point against his Adam's apple until a drop of blood appeared.

"Where are they taking the girl?" he asked.

The guard looked at him and then over at his partner.

"Fuck this shit. We're just guards. Ain't none of our fucking business." He looked up at Dick, "All I know

is there's a plane at Santa Monica Airport. It belongs to that Tigre dude."
   Dick pressed the point a little harder.
   "That's it man. That's all I know. Honest!"
   Treb could see it was true. "Let em go," he said.
   They let the two men up. After they were out the door and heading towards the driveway they could be heard bitching at each other.
   "Yeah, sure. Easy money. Just sit up here and watch the naked girls play around the pool and do drugs. Yeah, sure ... Asshole!"

Bob Bitchin

24

The small plane landed on the dirt strip outside of Puntarenas, Costa Rica. Eva woke up as the wheels hit the ground and started the plane bouncing. Her hands were tied behind her so she's been sleeping on her side. She ached and she still didn't have any idea where they were or where they were taking her.

Tirantia had piloted the plane all the way from Santa Monica and he was tired. The small plane had to stop every thousand miles for fuel, and its top speed was just under 175 miles an hour. The trip took just over twenty three hours. With the excitement of the escape from Armando's house he was exhausted. He thought back to when the firing began and it almost made him feel like he were back in the jungles of Nicaragua with El Jeffe, and that added even more to his fatigue.

The plane slowed as he reached the end of the small strip and he cut the engines. There was a Jeep waiting for him. Rabbit Moriega and Jake Simms were waiting in it. They started the Jeep and drove to where the plane stopped.

Tirantia opened the door and saw them sitting in the Rover watching him. He could tell something was wrong.

"Who's the girl?" Rabbit asked as he approached the plane. "What's the matter, not enough talent down here?" He wasn't smiling as he talked.

"Not like this," Tirantia said. "This is more special than anything you could imagine."

Simms walked over and grabbed her by the hair, turning her face up so they could see it.

"What are you talking about?" he said. "She's pretty, but so what? What's the deal?"

There was a tension in the air that Tirantia felt. Almost an electricity.

"What's the problem? You guys seem tense. What's up?" he asked.

"I'll tell you the fucking problem, asshole," Simms said taking out his Walther 9 mm and aiming it right at Tirantia's heart," you were planning on cutting us out. You figured it was easier to divide seven million by one then by three, right?"

Tirantia had been through to much to be shaken easily. He reached up and pushed the gun away, walking over to where the girl sat.

"You Gringos have been playing in the sun too long. You're imagining things," he said, as he untied Eva's hands and got her out of the plane. "What the fuck are you talking about?"

This time it was Rabbit speaking. "What were you doing on the other boat in Emerald Bay? You were supposed to be onshore watching the goods. No one was supposed to know you were there." He let that sink in and then continued. "What would El Jeffe have said if he'd seen you there? He'd know it was a setup. Maybe that's why everything got fucked up?"

"You guys have been watching too much American television," Tirantia smiled. "I wasn't crossing you, I was getting some insurance," and he pointed to Eva.

"Ok. Let's say for a minute you weren't fucking us over," Simms said," What's all this shit about insurance? Who the hell is this girl and why the hell did you bring her all the way down here?"

"You'll see," Tirantia said as he put Eva in the back seat of the Rover and jumped in next to her, "and you'll be glad I brought her. Now let's get over to the cabin. I need to set up a meeting with El Jeffe and I need some sleep."

Rabbit looked over at Simms and shrugged his shoulders.

"What the fuck?" said Simms, and Rabbit started the Jeep and headed away form the landing strip.

Across the Nicaraguan border there was a small camp set up in a dense jungle. There were four or five lean-tos made of canvas, one hut, and a couple of large tents. The largest was the field kitchen. A half dozen women were at work making vats full of beans and pounding the dough that would soon be pressed flat into the well known shape of the tortilla. Behind the tent a few more women worked pulling the feathers off of the four chickens that would be the evening meal.

In the hut El Jeffe was bent over some maps. A kerosene light burned over the table. Even though it was daylight the deep jungle cut out most of the daylight and the hut took away what was left. He reached down onto the map and flicked a large beetle off of Managua. Then he went back to studying the lines. Red lines showed where his men were in strength, blue showed where the government troops were strong. Most of the map was blue.

He sat back into a lone canvas chair. Besides the chair there was the table the map was laid out on and a small cot in the corner. Next to him was a small foot locker. It was all of his worldly possessions. He opened it and took out his last cigar, from Cuba.

He smiled and thought of the day that Fidel Castro had given him the box of Cuban cigars. As he bit off one end and started to chew on the other end he tried to remember how long ago that had been. Almost a year.

He knew his position was tenuous at best. The Americans kept trading him arms for drugs, and the Communists kept giving him drugs to give to the Americans. Being a simple man he didn't understand what it was all about, but as long as it kept him fighting to free the oppressed people he didn't care. How was he to know the Communists wanted the drugs to go to America. It was weakening the whole country. The more drugs that got in, the weaker the country became. Or so Castro thought.

He took out a match and lit the end of the big black stogie, inhaling the rich blue smoke deep into his lungs. He rested his head against the back of the chair and started to daydream. He wanted to enjoy his last cigar. It would probably be his last for a long time.

"El Jeffe!" a voice said from outside the hut. He sat up and cut the burned end off his cigar, tucking what was left into his shirt pocket.

"Yes, come in," he said.

A messenger came with an envelope and handed it to him, standing at very stiff attention while he waited to see if there would be an answer.

"Go get yourself something to eat," Heffe told the man," then return here in half an hour. I may have a message for you to take back."

As the man left the hut, El Jeffe opened the envelope. It was from his second in command. Jose Tirantia. He read it.

"It is urgent I meet with you as soon as possible. Meet me at A-7, noon tomorrow. Confirm. Tigre."

He looked at the map on his table and found A-7. There should be no problem getting there for the meeting.

El Jeffe knew it had to have something to do with the last shipment of cocaine that was supposed to be traded to the Americans for new rifles and badly needed ammunition. Something had gone wrong on the other end, but he didn't know what.

What, he wondered, does Tirantia want?

El Jeffe considered the proposed meeting. He had gone to the meeting point off the coast of California, as Tirantia had instructed him to. He didn't like leaving the country and his primary job, which was to stop the atrocities being inflicted by the Sandinistas, but Tigre insisted, and he trusted him.

When the boat they were to meet on had blown up he knew there was something very wrong. He instructed his captain to head out immediately. It would have been very difficult to explain his presence in the country.

As they rounded West End he had time to consider all the possibilities. The explosion would bring authorities. Once the authorities came in they would want to know who was on the other boats. The power boat had a chance to make it back to the mainland and the man he was supposed to meet could get lost over there, but El Jeffe wasn't supposed to be anywhere near the country. A speed boat could have caught them in a matter of a few hours, and radar would have kept them in sight.

It was then he told the Captain of the *Stone Witch* to

head in close to the rocks as they came around West End. Then El Jeffe walked to the back of the boat and pulled the release pin on the cargo, watching it sink to the bottom, well away from where the ship would settle. No on, not even the Captain knew where it was.

He went into the cabin and instructed the Captain to hit a rock and scuttle the boat once they were around the other side of the point. The Captain had made many runs up there from Nicaragua and was prepared for this. He had papers saying he was an American as well as another set showing him as Nicaraguan. El Jeffe checked his own second set of papers. Then he took the electronic release device and went into the galley. He placed it in a small plastic bag with a handful of salt. He taped it up carefully and wrapped it many more times taking a couple of lead weights from the fishing gear and placed them into another plastic bag. Then he put the switch in with them taping it tightly.

The Captain hailed him saying they were about to hit the rock. El Jeffe checked the shore. They were just halfway between a small rock and the shoreline. El Jeffe judged his position, paying special attention to a colored outcropping of rock on the shore, and dove into the water.

As he came close to the shore he checked his position carefully and dove down. The water was ten feet deep where he dove, and he found a nook to jam the sender into. Then he swam ashore and started the long walk back to Avalon. He was almost seen twice, but his many years of combat training in the jungle kept him hidden.

A week later he was back in Nicaragua. He notified his CIA contacts, Moriega and Simms, and waited for more news.

Now Tirantia wanted a meeting. He wrote a

Emerald Bay

message confirming the meet, and sealed it. A half hour later the messenger returned and picked it up.

There was small hut in the clearing. It looked deserted as El Jeffe's Jeep pulled up in front. His driver took a rifle with him as he checked the hut and made sure it was clear. Then he returned.

"Everything is as it should be," the man said, and he climbed back into the Jeep.

El Jeffe got out and walked to the entrance, checking his watch. It was 5 minutes until 12. Tirantia was always on time. He prided himself on that. Heffe chuckled to himself as he pictured his friend Tigre waiting down the road so as to arrive at the appointed time.

He signaled the driver to pull out of sight, and entered the hut. The interior was dark in contrast to the bright sun outside. The palm fronds of the palapa roof kept it cool. The walls were also palm fronds, and two windows set to the north and south allowed a cooling breeze. Heffe walked over to the small table against one wall and pulled an old wooden chair out. He sat back in it and out his feet on the table. He looked at his watch again. It was a Rolex. Tigre had given it to him three years ago after a trip to arrange for arms in Switzerland. The watch said it was noon, and as he'd expected, he heard a jeep pull up in front of the hut.

He put his feet down and got out of the chair. He walked over to the door and jus before he got there Tirantia walked in. He had a girl with him. She was wearing tight Levi's and a white loose fitting cotton shirt that showed an almost perfect figure. She looked American by her dress, but Spanish by her features. El Jeffe looked at her and thought there was something familiar about her, but couldn't place what it was.

If he hadn't spent his whole life in the jungle, if he

had been where there were mirrors, he would have known what it was.

The girl looked at him, and he could see confusion in her eyes. She had spent a lot of time in front of mirrors, and El Jeffe's deep blue/green eyes almost stopped her in her tracks.

Tirantia said, "El Jeffe my friend, this is Eva Analisia Ortiz from Chichetenango...she is your daughter." And he walked over and sat down at the small wooden table.

25

The long black limo pulled out onto the airport tarmac and cruised the small airstrip from front to back. At last they stopped in front of an old building. The sign in front was faded and two of the four spotlights on it were out. It said "Dutchman's Charters". Next to the small building there was a phone booth. Treb got out of the car and walked over to it.

"Hey Dick, you got a quarter? Fucking thing won't work without one," he shouted.

"Yeah, here," he said, walking from the car to the phone booth. "What the hell we doing here anyway? They're not here and we don't even know where they were going."

"I don't know. Maybe Fox found out something. That's who I'm calling."

He dialed the number and waited. Then he spoke.

"Bob, this is Treb, anything new on Eva?"

He listened intently. Dick watched as his face clouded over. It was obvious he didn't like what he was hearing. He listened for a long time. After awhile his grim face broke into a smile. Then he spoke again.

"Yeah, but how the hell did you hear about that? It just happened a little while ago," and he was silent again. He listened for a couple more minutes and then handed the phone to Dick saying, "Here, Mia wants to talk to you before we go."

Dick took the phone looking bewildered. "Go where?" he asked no one in particular and he put the phone to his ear. Treb walked back to the limo and sat down.

"Franko," he said, "One last favor. Can you take us to LAX? We gotta get to Nicaragua."

Franko just stared at him through the mirror.

On the way to LAX Franko left the intercom on and listened as Treb and Dick compared notes.

"Well what the fuck do you think of that?" Treb said, shaking his head, "that old fart your girlfriend works for is ex-CIA. I can't believe all the shit he found out with just a couple of phone calls."

"Sure would have helped knowing that before we went and played Rambo at the shack up in Beverly Hills," Dick replied.

"Hey. Come on Homeboy, you loved it. I haven't seen so much life in yer dead ass since we rousted those two hookers in DC and convinced 'em we were Feds. Admit it! This good life is for the fuckin birds. I was about to go and check into *Seizure World*. If it wasn't for those fuckin greaseballs grabbing Eva, I'd almost welcome a little diversion. What the fuck, you starting to get old on me?"

"Hey, I didn't see you climbing up the sides of no building back there. Yeah, sure, 'I'll take the back door.' " Dick laughed. "In the old days you'd a made your own back door. Face it,. fuck face, you're the one getting old!"

They both laughed as the adrenaline finally dissipated in their bodies. The rush of danger and exertion had actually gotten them high, and now they were starting to mellow out some.

"They got Phillipo, too. Guess old Fox ain't as old as we made em out to be," Dick said. "It seems he 'convinced' Phillipo to talk by giving him mass quantities of knuckle sandwiches. Mia couldn't believe it."

Treb sat back in the comfortable seat and looked at Dick.

"Look , I know I probably couldn't keep your ass here on a bet, but I gotta say it. You and Mia have something good going. You don't need this shit in your life. You could stay here and help by keeping Bob working on leads. You don't have to fly down to this mosquito infested jungle with me. Eva's mine, and I can get help if I need it."

Dick looked at him. They had been through a lot, and he loved the man.

"Fuck you," was all he said. They rode the rest of the way in silence.

After Franko dropped the two men off at the terminal he pulled the limo out into the traffic circle that went through the airport. The sun was just coming over the buildings. It had been a long night. He headed up Century Boulevard and pulled into the gas station at Century and Aviation. While the attendant filled the tank Franko dialed a number on the phone in the booth.

"This is Barentelli. Let me speak to Farmer." He watched the man clean the windshield on the limo as he waited.

"Farmer, this is Frank Barentelli. What the hell happened last night? I gave you the info in plenty of time for you guys to stop all that shooting before it began. What the hell am I doing out here taking a chance on getting offed by these sleaze balls if the info I get is ignored by you assholes?"

Frank Barentelli had been working undercover with the Omega Squad for almost three years, ever since he was busted by the DEA for possession for sales of cocaine. He'd done time twice before for armed robbery and assault, and this would have been his third conviction. He was easy to turn. His position in the Warriors made him valuable to the Omega Squad. They had been trying to infiltrate the club for years.

He listened to the control agent explain to him that they actually wanted the bikers to take down Armando.

"Well, it's none of my fucking business anyway," he said with a touch of bitterness in his voice. "Anyway," he continued, "I just dropped Lincoln and Bondano off at Avianca Airlines. They are flying down to Costa Rica to try and find the broad. Thought you ought to know."

Back in the car he turned the radio on as he pulled out onto the 405 Freeway heading back to Buena Park. He listened to the news on the radio and had to laugh.

"Last night a small fire broke out at the home of a well known financier in Beverly Hills," the announcer said. "Three people who were asleep in the home died in that fire. Neighbors said they thought they heard what sounded like gunshots, but some fireworks were found in the garage and that accounted for the noise... Meanwhile traffic on the Pasadena Freeway..."

Flight 289 from Los Angeles to San Jose, Costa Rica would take about four and a half hours, so Treb and Dick would have some time to try and figure out what they were going to do and get some rest. While most of the people on the plan e were watching the latest movie , "Rocky 7 meets Superman 6" they sat and discussed their possibilities.

"Fox found out that she was taken by Tirantia, which we knew. What we didn't know is, he was with the Contras. It seems our government, in their infinite wisdom, was using him to trade drugs for arms for the Contras."

"He was the guy that had the CIA blow the boat that killed Karen and Rom," Treb continued, his eyes hazing a little as he remembered the explosion.

Now Dick knew why Treb had been so upset talking to Fox on the phone before they left.

"Also," he went on, "he was connected with Eva's old "sponsor", that Huntington guy. Seems his remains were found by a fishing boat in the Catalina Channel a couple of months after the explosion. They never announced it. Their men in Central America said it was just supposed to be a meeting and told them not to bust it up but the CIA thinks there was something being exchanged at that meeting, and that things went wrong. They don't know what."

The stewardess brought over a couple of fresh drinks. Treb waited until she was gone, and then went on.

"The one thing we don't know is why this guy Tigre, or Tirantia, wanted Eva. That's the bugger in this deal."

Dick took a sip from his Bloody Mary and looked at Treb.

"Maybe it's love," he said.

"Yeah, right," Treb replied, and took a long swig out of his drink.

"Well, in a little while we're going to be landing in San Jose. What are we going to do when we get there?" Dick asked. "Costa Rica is a big country, and we won't have any guns."

"I'm not real sure yet. We're gonna play it by ear to start. Fox said there were two men down here that are working for his old CIA partner Miles Kirkland. If we get stuck he said to contact them."

"How do we find em?" Costa Rica is a small country, but not that small," Dick asked.

"He said it wouldn't be hard. They're in a fishing village on the west coast, Puntarenas. It shouldn't be hard to find two gringos."

Dick asked," Did he give you any names?"

"Yeah," said Treb," Simms and Moriega."

Dick's mouth dropped open, "Rabbit?" and he took a long hard drink.

Dick was troubled as the plane passed over San Salvador and headed south to pass over Managua. In his thought/sleep he was on another plane flying on the other side of the world, passing over Hue to a dropping point just below the town of Quang Tri in North Vietnam.

His squad of ten men was to drop behind the lines and work their way south back to their own front, causing as much havoc as possible. It was Dick's eighth drop, and his last. He tightened the straps on his chute when the red light came on and the buzzer started. Captain Robert "Rabbit" Moriega stood at the door. Dick was a sergeant and his second in command. The jump master watched the pilot and co-pilot and on their command pointed at Moriega. He was the first out the door. Dick checked his watch and counted the other 8 men out at five second intervals, then he followed. His heart jumped as he felt the wind hit him when he cleared the door. No matter how many times he jumped, each time was a whole new experience.

It was dark, and he hated night jumps. The jungle below was black. he couldn't tell if he was going to land on a tree top or in a field. In the darkness he could make out most of the other chutes as they dropped below him.

All of a sudden there was a tree, and his chute caught in one of the upper branches. It swung him hard into the tree trunk. The blow knocked the air out of him and slammed his arm into his side, breaking two ribs.

He blacked out.

When he came around his side hurt so bad he wanted to scream, but he didn't. He looked at his watch. He had been out for around fifteen minutes. They were together at the meeting point within 8 minutes after the jump. Now he'd have to find them in the jungle.

But first he had to get down.

He studied the way the chute was draped and saw there was no way he could untangle it. He swung to a strong branch and when he had a good grip released the chute. His full weight dropped onto the branch and he heard it creak, but it didn't break. He tried to work the chute down so it wouldn't be spotted, but couldn't free it so he did the next best thing. He folded as much of it as he could. Climbing to almost the top of the tree to do so. Once it was as small as he could get it he cut a couple of the lines and used them as a double drop rope. He threw one side over the highest branch he could reach and tied the other end to his body. Then he lowered himself to the ground. Once he was down he pulled the rope over the branch and rolled it up, tying it together and looping it over his shoulder in case he needed it later.

His side hurt more as he ran to where the meeting was supposed to be. As he got close he slowed and listened. About a hundred yards away he heard voices. When he heard it was English he started towards the voices. He kept low and in the bushes and came in as close as he could. When he came up on them he saw they weren't alone.

In a small clearing there were 6 of his team. Rabbit was standing trying to talk to the Viet Cong that seemed to be in charge. He knew a little English, but not enough to converse.

"Look you punk motherfucker," Rabbit was saying, smiling, in a voice that sounded sweet and smooth, "We are lost, you see? We look for McDonald's. We good. Australian, no American. Yes, Rice Breath?"

It was obvious the man didn't understand, and even more, he didn't care. He had two of the guards take a man over to an edge of the clearing. It was then Dick understood what was going on. The three missing men were laying there. They had no clothes on and they were dead.

The guard took the new man to the edge and told him to strip. They tore his clothes off, taking his shoes, his watch and school ring. Then, without even a glance, one of the guards put a pistol to his head and pulled the trigger. The sound was dull and sickening. The man's body dropped to the ground and they dragged him to where the others lay.

Dick looked around the clearing and counted the VC. There were about fifteen of them. Three or four were over by where the bodies lay, going through the dead men's clothes that was stacked there.

He knew he didn't have much time to make a plan. If all the men were killed there was no way he could ever get back to his lines, and it looked like they were killing a man about every three or four minutes to make the ones that were left suffer more.

He worked his way back to where the men were going through the clothes when he got there he saw they were blocked from the view of the rest of the guards by some bushes.

Without thinking, using reflexes more than a plan he came up behind one of the men and chopped at the base of his neck with his full strength. Before the man ever started to fall he rammed his hand straight across to the nearest man's face, breaking his nose and jamming the broken bone into the man's brain.

The other two men turned to see what was happening but it was already too late. Dick's training in Martial Arts had been almost since birth, and he moved with such speed his limbs were near invisible. He spun a kick into the groin of one of the men and jammed his open hand into the last mans solar plexus. The four men were dead in less than fifteen seconds.

Dick pulled the bodies into the brush and moved around to where he could see what was happening. Two guards were bringing another man over to be executed.

He knew it was now or never. Rabbit was looking at the leader whose back was to Dick. He watched his man being led away to be shot, and as he did he saw a small movement in the bush. Dick saw the recognition in Rabbit's eyes when he saw him and lifted his finger to his mouth telling him not to give him away. Rabbit understood instantly and looked away. As he glanced back trying to be nonchalant he saw Dick tap his watch and hold up 10 fingers. He would understand 10 seconds, because in 10 minutes all the men would have been dead.

Dick counted off seven seconds. It seemed like an eternity. Then he came out of the bushes slamming a side kick into the guard on the left and spinning with a spin kick to the other man's face.

Just as the other guards started to turn and see what the commotion was, Rabbit and the remaining three men took out the three closest guards. Dick and

Robbins, the man who was on his way to the grave, ran and jumped the two guards nearest them. Dick had his .45 out as soon as his man dropped. Now that there was no more surprise he didn't need to keep quiet. He dropped to his stomach after he hit his man and brought the weapon up, the pain from his broken ribs almost making him pass out. He shot by reflex action, putting a hole in one man's head, and then dropping another just as the man raised his gun. The remaining three men didn't have a chance. The prisoners of a minute earlier were now the captors. The three guards died fast.

The remaining force of five men stripped all the weapons off the dead men, and then gathered their own weapons.

Rabbit looked at Dick.

"What took ya so fucking long?" he asked, and then he wrapped his arms around him and hugged him so hard his broken ribs almost made him pass out again. "I was never so happy to see anyone in my whole fucking life. You'll get the CMH for this or I'll die trying to get it for you."

Dick came out of his sleep-dream-thought with that on his mind. *I thought he did die trying? I thought I killed him!*

The intercom on the plane announced they would be landing on San Jose in ten minutes. He sat up and looked over at Treb. The big man was asleep. Dick reached over to him and shook his arm.

"Hey, Goombah, better get ready for action, we're about to land."

26

Eva slowly woke from a deep sleep and rubbed her eyes. She looked around the small room they'd locked her in. The floor was concrete and dirty. The walls were made from bricks of the local mud. A small window was on one wall, but it was boarded up. It was dark. The one door was made of wood, and it was very old. The wood was gray with age.

Why am I here?, she wondered to herself, and who is that man they say is my father?

She'd slept for almost 18 hours straight after being locked up in the tiny room. She could tell from the slant of the sunlight streaking down through the Palapa roof that it was late afternoon. The heat was unbearable.

My father! He can't be my father. He's dead. My mother told me he was taken off to fight and was killed. That was why he never came home and why they never married. How can he be here in Costa Rica?

Her mind followed all the logical routes, and each time she came to the same conclusion. In her head she knew he couldn't be her father. In her heart she knew he was. Looking into his eyes was the same as looking into a mirror.

That first minute in the small cabin had shocked her considerably. She walked in out of the bright sun into a darkened room, and there he was. Then Tirantia telling the man she was his daughter.

What a shock! He looked more surprised than me. Didn't he know he had a daughter?

The moment only lasted a few seconds. Then a man took her by the arm and took her back to the jeep. He tied her wrist to the windshield brace and drove off. She was still in shock. He brought her to the cabin she was now in and locked her into the small room. She went instantly into a troubled sleep.

Now that she was awake things were starting to clear in her head. Now she knew why she'd been taken and brought all the way here. It was obvious Tirantia wanted something from the man he said was her father. She was being used as a lever.

She felt nothing for the man who'd left her mother pregnant and unmarried almost 20 years ago. How could she feel anything except possibly hate? To be brought up as a bastard in a religious community was very hard on her, and it was equally hard on her mother to be an unwed mother. No, they owed this man nothing.

But then again, she thought, if it really is my father? She could hear talking in the room on the other side of the door. It was the man who'd brought her here and another guard. Her eyes wandered over the room.

Other than the door and the window there were no other openings. She got up and stretched, brushing the dirt off her Levi's, then walked over to the window. She pulled on the boards but they were tight and strong.

The only furniture in the room was a three legged stool. She picked it up and carried it to the corner of the room where the roof came down the lowest. It was about 7 feet from the floor to the roof. She stood on the stool and lifted the corner of the palm frond palapa roof. It was as she expected. The roof was just tied down with hand woven hemp. She took off her small necklace and looked at the charm. It was the gold plated sea shell Treb had bought her when they first were together. She didn't have time to dwell on the thoughts that went through her mind. She missed Treb and wished he were there. How was he doing? Did he know where she was?

She used the edge of the shell and cut the hemp. Then she moved the stool over and cut the next three in line on each side of where the roof met the corner of the room. At last it was loose enough to lift almost a foot. Plenty of room for her to slip through it if she could get up there.

She moved the stool to the very corner and stood up on her toes. She could easily reach the top of the wall, but she would have to pull herself up to get through the small opening. Again her mind wandered to Treb, and she silently thanked him for taking her to the gym with him each day. Pulling herself up and slipping through the opening was easier than the she thought. The only hard part was keeping it quiet so as not to alarm the guards.

As she hoisted herself on top of the wall she looked out from under the roof. There was no one outside.

Then she swung down on the other side and hung down until her feet touched.

As soon as she was on the ground she ran into the jungle nearest the house. She kept running as long as she had breath, breaking through brush and undergrowth as she went. Her white cotton shirt had small tears in it, but she didn't even notice. She just wanted to get away.

When she couldn't run anymore she collapsed and lay there catching her breath and trying to put things together.

She knew she was in Costa Rica somewhere near the Nicaragua border, she'd heard the guards talking about going over to the 'camp' for lunch, and she knew the camp was across the border.

The more she lay there the more her thoughts went back to her mother. A lot of it was because of her surroundings. She'd spent the first fourteen years of her life in the jungles of Guatemala. Laying there all of the city life was suddenly like a bad dream. Once again she was girl in the jungles of her homeland. There was no fear. Just a feeling of being at home.

In a couple of seconds her mind was made up. She wanted to go home. Not home to Catalina, but home to her mother.

She looked up through the dense undergrowth at the position of the sun. It was setting. By its position she knew which way she had to go, and she started to walk north. She had to find a road or landmark.

She followed a small path as it wound to the northeast. Every once and awhile she would stop and listen to see if guards had discovered she was missing and were following her. As it got darker she felt safer. She walked for hours, and soon the small path started to get wider and more used. Other paths intersected and crossed and she kept heading north-east.

Somewhere around midnight she saw some lights

ahead and worked her way around a small village. There were just three or four huts, but she had a bad feeling about it. She could see a man sitting by the small fire in the middle of the huts, and she knew if they were bandits she wouldn't stand much of a chance.

By dawn she had covered only about seven or eight miles. She didn't know it, but she was just about on the Nicaragua-Costa Rica border. She was tired and hungry. She searched for a safe place to rest, and found a clump of bushes that were off the path and looked safe. In a few minutes she was asleep.

When she woke it was near noon. The sun beat down and she ached all over. The heat of the day was almost unbearable, and the humidity was stifling. She may have felt at home in the jungle, but all those years of air conditioned luxury made her unsuited for the jungle weather. She was covered with small cuts wherever her clothing didn't cover, and she was very lonely.

The rest of the day she spent alternately walking and resting. She would follow the path, always heading north-east, usually for an hour or so. Then she would rest for ten or fifteen minutes, and continue. Water and food was plentiful. She'd eat some bananas and other fruits to keep up her strength, and kept moving.

About seven in the evening, just before sunset, she came on a paved road. It was narrow but paved, so she knew it had to have some sort of public transportation. In most Central American countries the bus systems were better run then the ones in the US, even if the buses weren't exactly the best.

She walked along the side of the road for a little less than an hour and she heard the telltale banging of a bus coming up behind her. She turned and flagged it down, The sign on the front read "Managua."

The bus was just as she remembered them. It was

painted red and green and black with decals stuck all over it. It was probably a retired school bus from the United States. Made to hold 36 passengers but never running with less than fifty people on board.

She squeezed her way into the crowded bus and spoke with the bus driver. All she had was some American money still in her pocket. He was more than happy to take an American dollar for the fare. It was normally 300 pesos, or about 20 cents. She pushed her way back and found a place to stand, holding onto a seat back to balance herself as the bus lurched into life.

Across from her was a family looking at her. The father was small and frail, and looked to be about thirty, but his skin was weathered like that of a man seventy years old. His wife was just as bedraggled, and their three children sat with eyes large and round, looking at Eva.

She reached into her shirt and pulled out two bananas she still had on her. She handed them to the children. They hesitated and looked at their mother, and when she smiled they took it.

"Muchas gracias," they chimed, and grubby faces broke into bright and sunny smiles.

Soon a portion of seat was vacated and Eva sat down. She considered her situation. Soon she would be in Managua. From there she knew it was about 250 miles to Chechetenango in Guatemala. First she had to cut across a section of Honduras and through El Salvador. With bus service like it was, it should take a little over a day. Not too bad.

As the bus rolled on, stopping at small crossroads and paths every mile or so, Eva moved until she was sitting against a wall. She leaned against the window looking out at the passing country, and soon she was asleep.

27

The San Jose Airport was crowded as Treb and Dick walked off the plane and into the sweltering heat. The passengers were guided like sheep through some turnstiles and then to their waiting luggage. Since Treb and Dick had no luggage they went straight to Aduana, or customs.

Neither of them had passports, so they soon found themselves sitting in a small overheated office with a self important bureaucrat staring at them from across a battered desk.

Treb handed the man his wallet opened to the driver's license, it had a twenty dollar bill folded half and tucked next to it. The man looked at it and took the bill.

"Your driver's license seems to be enough identification, sir," he smiled, "but next time, please to observe formalities of a passport I hope your friend's license is just as good." He held out his hand for Dick's wallet.

"Ah yes," the man said, "no problem. I will have two visas for you in a minute. Please wait outside."

In fifteen minutes they were walking out the front of the terminal with valid visas. They stepped over to a cab and asked the diver in Spanish how much it would be to take them to Puntarenas. $30 American was set and soon they were heading down the mountain from the capital city of San Jose to the small Pacific Coast town.

The road between the Capital and Puntarenas was wide and paved, and the taxi made good time. The two men stared out the window a they passed through some of the densest jungle in the world.

"I hope she's alright," Treb said to break the silence.

"Look," said Dick, "it's obvious that this guy wanted her for something, he sure as hell didn't take her for ransom, right?"

"Yeah," Treb replied, "but what the hell would he want her for? It has to have something to do with that asshole she used to live with. I can't picture her in that life, but I know she was there. This just doesn't make sense."

"Well, we know she was brought to Puntarenas, and we know the guy that took her is with the Contras," Dick went on," all we have to do is use the facts we know and a little logic. Fact one; they will have either landed or soon will be landing in or near Puntarenas. A small plane has to take at least three times as long as a commercial jet. By the time we get there they should still be within a few miles unless they plan on flying from there."

"Ok, so all we have to do is find them within a couple hundred miles of jungle," Treb laughed. "What the fuck. It should be easy."

Dick was glad to see Treb could laugh about it. He was getting back to normal.

They rode in silence for awhile.

"Hey Dick," Treb asked about an hour later, "how come you know this guy Moriega? How'd you know his name was Rabbit?"

"Bro, I'll tell you what. If this is the same Moriega then he's a ghost. I killed him in Vietnam twenty-eight years ago."

Dick told Treb about his last drop in Vietnam and how it went wrong from the start.

"After we offed the first group of VC we ran into three more large patrols. By the time we were near our own lines there were just two of us left. Rabbit and me. I thought he was the best man I'd ever known."

"So what happened? Why'd you have to off him?"

Dick noticed the way Treb had said "Have to". There was no way he would even think Dick would have done something bad. It made him smile.

"While we were waiting to be shipped home we were pulling some guard duty at the airfield in Saigon." Dick went on. "One night I was on watch and I noticed a couple of guys where they shouldn't have been. They were loading something onto a plane that was to leave for the states the next morning. When I told them to hold it they ran. I shot both of them before they were twenty feet away. The other guard said they were dead as a doornail, and there was no way they couldn't have been."

"What's that got to do with Rabbit? It sounds like he was an alright type," Treb asked.

"One of the men was Rabbit. They were loading 200 pounds of heroin on the plane."

215

Dick sat back and was silent. The rest of the trip went without words. Both men were lost in their own world.

When the taxi pulled off the highway and into the town, Treb told the driver to stop at the first bar. It was as good a place as any to start looking. They got out and paid the driver. Then they looked around as he pulled away. The main street had six or seven bars, and an equal amount of hotels. They walked over to a place called "Diablo's" and went in through the front door.

It was wide open inside with just a few tables scattered around. They all had dirty table cloths draped on them and there was a long bar against one wall. A woman in her forties stood behind the bar and nodded to them as they came in. They walked over and took a coupled of stools near the center of the bar.

They ordered a drink and looked around.

"Do you know a couple of gringo's that live here?" he asked the woman behind the bar. "Simms and Moriega?"

The woman just looked at them as if she were deaf. Treb knew his Spanish was good enough to be understood, so he reached into his pocket and pulled out a twenty.

"Simms and Moriega?" he asked again.

This time she seemed to understand.

"One dark and tall, the other a little heavier?" she asked.

Treb didn't know what they looked like, but he nodded yes.

"Si," she said, "I know of them."

"Where can we find them?" he asked her again.

Once more she looked at him as if she didn't understand. He took out another twenty and she smiled.

"Conchita's, two blocks that way," she pointed up the

street. She pocketed the bills and walked to the sink where she busied herself re-washing the same glass she was working on when they came in.

They finished their drinks and dropped a couple American dollars on the bar. Then they left.

As they approached Conchita's they saw that it was a bar on the lower level and had rooms above. It was one of the cleaner places in town. They walked in and took a seat at one of the tables in a corner. There was one other table occupied by two women who looked like they were permanent fixtures there.

The girl behind the bar walked over to get their order.

"Dos cervezas," he said," and we're looking for some friends of ours. Simms and Moriega. Are they here now?"

She looked at them for a minute and started to walk back to the bar.

"No, they left this morning in their Jeep."

Treb looked at Dick. "Guess we wait here."

"You want to get a room here?" Dick asked, "We might need one."

"No, let's wait and see what happens."

The cold beers were set down in front of them and they both took long drinks from the dark cold bottles.

Jake Simms wheeled the jeep off the highway and swung down the main street of town heading for their hotel. He was still pissed about what Tirantia had pulled and had a bad feeling that they were being cut out of the deal.

"So what do we do now?" Rabbit asked. "What if this guy tried to cut us out?"

"Nothing," smiled Simms. "nothing at all. We'll let our 'friends' handle it on the other end. If he thinks he can get away cutting us out, he'd better think again. If we're not in on it, no one is, agreed?"

"Yeah, I guess so," Rabbit didn't sound so sure. He had hoped this would be the deal that would retire him once and for all. He was getting tired.

The jeep was left outside Conchita's and the two men walked into the bar.

"Let's have a drink," Rabbit said. "I need one."

They walked to the bar and sat down. As they did Simms noticed the two gringos sitting at the corner table. He sat so he could see them in the mirror. One was as big as a house and scary looking. The other was just scary. He nudged Rabbit and nodded at the mirror.

Just as Rabbit looked up he saw a face from the past. At first he was so glad to see someone from the 'good days' he jumped up and turned as if to embrace his old friend. The look on Dick's face stopped him cold in his tracks.

Before either of them could move the man was where they were sitting ,and as Rabbit turned towards him, Dick slammed a right hook under his jaw, knocking him off his stool.

Simms and Treb both just stared. Simms didn't have any idea of what was going on, and Treb was just plain surprised.

Rabbit was the most surprised. Even more so when Dick helped him off the floor, held him at arm's length and called him a dirty motherfucker, and then hugged him and started slapping him on the back.

"You asshole!" Dick went on, "I thought I killed your ass. What the fuck was the idea, anyway? You have any idea of the shit I went through because of wasting you?"

The two of them walked off to another table leaving Treb and Simms standing slack jawed and staring after them

Treb turned to Simms.

"You must be Jake Simms. My name's Treb Lincoln.

Miles Kirkland told me to look you up. Said you might be able to help me."

Simms took the big man's hand and sat back, keeping an eye on his partner at the other table.

"What the hell was all that about?" Simms asked Treb as he picked up his beer and downed it.

"They were together in 'Nam," he said, signaling the girl to bring a couple more beers." Guess their going over old times or something."

"Musta been a violent group over there, huh?"

Simms looked at the man sitting next to him. He was huge and none of it was fat. His arms looked like meatloaves sticking out of his sleeves. He didn't look like he was with 'the company'.

But on the other hand, Miles Kirkland was the head of Covert Operations, and there was no way he'd give out a man's real name and location to someone that wasn't with them.

"What's your stat?" he asked the big man. Stat was the company way of asking for a sign or counter sign to identify each other.

"What the fuck's a stat?" the man asked.

Now Simms was real confused.

Over at the table Rabbit and Dick were in deep conversation.

"As soon as I heard your name I figured it had to be a setup back in Nam," Dick was saying, "but I knew I nailed your ass to the cross. How the fuck'd they do that one?"

"Blanks," Rabbit smiled, reaching over and grabbing Dick's forearm. "God damn blanks." He hesitated, "Jesus Christ , it's good to see you. I haven't been this happy since I left Nam, you fuckhead!"

"What the hell are you doing down here? You with the company too?"

Rabbit knew he didn't have to be cautious with dick, and even if he was supposed to be, he didn't care. He was just glad to see him.

"No," Dick answered," as a matter of fact we're looking for a girl."

"Well shit," Rabbit smiled broadly," no problem. You want tall, short, skinny, or fat!"

"No, we're looking for a particular girl. A friend of ours told us to contact you. Said if there was any problem for you to call Kirkland and use the word 'Foxfire' and he'd verify everything."

"Shit man, I don't need to verify anything. Any man who kills me is friend for life. Let's have another brew," he said, and he waved at the bar girl.

Then his attitude seemed to shift.

"Foxfire? Are you sure he said Foxfire? I heard he died a few years ago. Never met him myself but he's a fucking legend around here." He seemed lost in thought for a minute, then he changed back to his old self and started asking questions again.

"So what's the deal on this girl. Must be some hot stuff for you to come searching. What's she up to, bringing in shit from Columbia?"

"No, she's my best friend's girlfriend," he said pointing at Treb.

It was the first time that Rabbit noticed who Dick had come in with. He looked over at the man and let out a low whistle.

"Doesn't look like that gorilla would need any help doing anything, how'd he lose her?"

"Some guy named 'Tigre' snatched her. You know him?"

"Tirantia," Rabbit said, and all of a sudden reality was back on him.

28

"How do I know she's my daughter, and even if she were, what difference would it make?" El Jeffe was saying to Tarantia.

"Heffe," the man replied , "you are an old woman. You have always been an old woman. You fight with a fear of killing. The younger men no longer want to follow you. They have no respect. You are soft. You talk of treaties and compromise." Tigre spat with disgust. "You have lost your huevos, your balls." He held his hands up to show his disgust.

"And so, my friend, now you have decided that you can run things better, is this so?" El Jeffe asked.

"Si, Heffe," he used the man's name as if it were acid

in his mouth, "much better. I am not afraid to show the people who has the strength and the might. All I need is the shipment which waits for us in Texas and you will see what real revolution is all about."

"And you think that I will give you the cocaine to trade for these arms, knowing what you plan with them?"

"You are a woman," he spat again, "and women have no place in war."

El Jeffe sat back in his chair and looked at his one time friend and one time right hand man. He shook his head slowly with disgust.

"You are wrong. You will see."

"You have one day to decide. I will return tomorrow at noon with the girl. Let us see if you have the huevos to watch your own flesh and blood die at your command."

With that Tirantia turned and walked out of the cabin, leaving the man sitting at the small table.

El Jeffe reached into his shirt pocket and took out the stub of a cigar he had managed to save. He took out a match and lit it, inhaling the blue white smoke.

His mind wandered. He found it did that a lot the older he got, and always back to when he was a very young man. The last time he was actually carefree. At 15 years of age he was little more than a boy, but in war torn Central America that was almost middle age.

He remembered the girl he was in love with, Marina Ortiz. She was still vivid in his mind after all of these years. In his mind he could see how the girl resembled her. She was a little taller than average, and she was 14 years old. They were waiting until the party for her fifteenth birthday, which was always a big affair in his village. Then he would ask for her hand. He remembered that she was heavy. Even at fourteen she weighed 165 pounds. To young Juanito, which was El Jeffe's given name as a young man, she was a dream.

They were so in love back then.
And Eva had her mother's looks and more, and she had her father's eyes.
He thought back to how they'd sneak away from the village. She would smile at him and wink as she went to the well to get water for her father's hut. He would look up from his chores, cutting wood or cleaning whatever animal his father had killed, and smile to her.
Then they would meet at 'their' tree just off the path that led to Chichetenango, the larger village a few kilometers away. They would follow a small path from there to their hideaway.
He could picture it. A very small clearing. Tall trees blocking the sun, but a small patch of short grass grew there to cushion them as they lay there. The river was dammed by a log that had fallen years ago blocking the river and making a deep spot. The water was always very cool and inviting. From the time they were children they had gone there to swim, only as they got older he started to feel funny when he'd see her naked getting in and out of the water.
The Padre said it was bad to look upon each other without clothes, but all he knew was how much he liked seeing her that way.
Just before the soldiers came to the village to take him away was when he was the happiest in his life. He was allowed to hunt with the men for the wild pig, which was an honor as old as the country itself. You were a man when you were invited on your first hunt.
When he'd returned for his first kill he remembered how proud she'd looked. The wink and nod were automatic and soon the two of them were in their private heaven. He remembered how soft and warm she felt. A few days later was the first time they made love.
Then the party celebrating her birthday. The whole village joined as she passed into womanhood. There

was dancing and music, and a pig was killed and roasted.

That night he went to her father. Now that he had killed his first wild pig he was a man, he was proud. He walked into her father's hut with his head held high.

When he left the plans were set. They would marry at the next full moon.

But his life was to change. Three days before the wedding the soldiers came. The war in El Salvador was at its height and all the young men were being taken. Even though he thought of himself as a Guatemalan, he could not shirk his duty. His roots were deep, and to the people of Central America there were no national borders. The Communists were starting to push them. In a few days he was deep in battle. He never returned to that village.

For years he fought. First with the forces in El Salvador, and then into Honduras, finally heading up the resistance in Nicaragua. It seemed there was always another fight. Another village that was being dominated. His people being killed and decimated.

He dropped the smoldering ash of his cigar to the floor of the hut and stood. It was time to act. He walked out into the fading sunlight and walked to his waiting Jeep. The driver saluted him as he boarded the vehicle, and started the engine, heading back to the compound.

Tirantia's Jeep pulled up in front of the cabin where Eva was being held. The two guards came to the door to meet him.

"Bring the girl!" he said, and he considered just how to best use his advantage.

From the first time he'd seen the girl in Armando's house he was sure it had to be El Jeffe's daughter. He remembered the many nights they'd spent in the jungles talking of the old days, and how Heffe talked of the girl in his village near Chichetenango. When he saw her eyes and found out she was from the same village he was sure and her age was right.

The guards came running out of the hut in a panic.

"Senor Tigre, she is gone!" one man shouted. The other looked frightened.

"Gone? What do you mean she's gone? Where did she go? How could se..?" he didn't finish the sentence. He left the jeep and ran into the hut, straight to the room she was held in. At a glance he saw the stool and the small opening where the roof had been pulled back.

He walked into the front room where the two men were standing. He pulled his Baretta out of its holster and put it in the larger man's forehead, pulling the trigger before the man could move.

The man's body dropped to the floor with a thud.

Then he turned on the other man.

"You have twenty hours in which to find the girl, or not only will you join your friend, but so will your family, understand?"

The man shook his head slowly. He was still in shock from seeing his boyhood friend die, but he realized he would live.

Tirantia walked out of the hut and around the back, he followed the girls' tracks as fast as he could, and saw the broken leaves and branches.

"She was in a big hurry. She leaves a trail a blind man could follow," he said to the man, "get two men and have them track her through the brush. You know what she looks like. There is no place for her to run, so she will head to her home. I am sure of it." He thought for a minute, then spoke more to himself than to the frightened man beside him.

"She could not do it on foot. Somewhere she will come to a road, and then she must either get a ride or get on a bus." He thought some more, and then continued. "If she is going home, north to Guatemala she will go through Managua. All roads pass through the city." He turned to the man beside him again, this time speaking louder , "We will take the Jeep and go t Managua, now! Stop at the village and get the two men to come back here and follow the trail."

    The bus hit a large chuckhole and Eva's head smacked against the window waking her from a restless sleep. As she woke the realities of where she was came back. She wished that Treb were here and all this was a bad dream, but as she looked out the window she realized this was her reality.
    They were passing through Managua, the capital city of Nicaragua. The streets looked like they were deserted, with an occasional child or old woman seen picking through the rubble. It looked as if it had been bombed out. She was amazed that anyone could live there.
    The bus bounce along the streets and headed towards the central market area. Even there, where all the commerce of the city was headquartered, it was like a war zone. Uniformed soldiers and men not in uniform all carried weapons.
    The bus pulled up in front of the small building that was used as a bus station and the people started to get off. Eva stood and tried to stretch. It had been a long and bumpy ride, and the events of the previous day and night had taken their toll.
    As she stepped off the bus she looked around the square. There were little girls carrying boxes filled with small plastic bags of juice singing out "Refrescas!" She bought one and stuck the little straw into the bag, sucking the sweet cool nectar into her dry mouth. She walked long the sidewalk looking at the nameplates on the buses that were there. Some were heading south

to Costa Rica and Panama, others were going east across Nicaragua to Prinzapolka and Huantan on the Caribbean side. As last she came to one that said San Salvador. That was almost two thirds of the way to her home. She asked the driver when it would be leaving and was told she had about fifteen minutes.

She wandered across the street to the Mercado to look at what was on display in the stalls and to use the restroom.

Ten minutes later she walked to the bus, carrying some chicken and fruit for the trip. Just as she was boarding the bus she saw Tirantia's face in the crowd. She turned and started to run. She went across the street and through the many stalls that were there. Looking back she saw Tirantia and one of the guards that had held her back at the small hut. She threw her packages to the ground and ran as fast as she could, dodging carts and people as she went. She ran around a corner and into an alley, heading to an open door near the end.

She turned into the door and ran right into the arms of the guard. He'd come around from the other side. Before she could run he grabbed her.

She fought him off as best as she could trying to remember what Dick had taught her, but soon Tirantia was there and he put his pistol into her side, pushing hard.

"Shut up and do as I say," he snarled.

Later she was sitting in the front seat of the Jeep as they passed south out of Managua. The guard sat in back holding the weapon on her, and Tirantia drove.

Bob Bitchin

29

Rabbit was more confused now then he'd been in his entire life. When Dick walked back into his life all of a sudden his plans for early retirement seemed soiled. He sat in a pool of guilt as he heard what happened when the bomb that he'd planted destroyed so many lives.

All his life since Vietnam he'd been involved in this type of violence, but it never seemed to hit so close to home. He was always distant from the results. Now here, sitting in a sleazy bar deep in Costa Rica, listening to a man who had once saved his life talk about how he'd killed one of his best friends and an innocent woman on her wedding day.

He glanced at his partner, Jake Simms, trying to think of what was going through his mind. Did he feel the same guilt, or was it just water off a duck's back?

"So you see," Treb was saying, "it's important that we find Eva and find her fast. Do you have any idea why this man wanted her so bad? Any idea at all?"

Rabbit wanted to tell them that he knew where she probably was, but one look at Simms told him not to. All he had to do now was decided where his real priorities lay. With his partner or with a man who had risked his life many years ago to save his.

Simms responded to Treb's question with another question.

"How do you know this Tigre wants to harm her? Maybe there's another reason he took her. This is a big country and she could be hard to find, right Rabbit?" his partner looked at him with a smile.

"Jake," he said, "did you know 'foxfire' when he was down here?"

The man hesitated and looked quickly at Rabbit.

"Foxfire? No. He was Kirkland's partner wasn't he, before Miles took over as head of the department? What's he got to do with this?"

"Foxfire is the authorization, through Miles himself. This isn't just another information dig. This is from the top. Shouldn't we...?" Rabbit let the sentence drop.

The question wasn't missed by Treb or Dick. They could see there was something going on. The two men knew something and weren't talking.

Treb was starting to lose it. He looked at these two men who were down here playing in people's lives as if they were games. All of a sudden he reached across the table and grabbed Simms by the collar and almost lifted him across the table. Rabbit started to move to protect his partner but Dick was too fast. He grabbed his arm in midair and whipped it around behind him, in a hammerlock.

"Rabbit," Dick said, "don't you fucking think about moving or I'll break it off and jam it so far up your ass you'll need to yawn to scratch your ass, you got me?"

Rabbit relaxed and sat back.

"Okay you assholes," Treb said to Simms, "this is the deal as I see it. You pricks know where Eva is, or at least where Tigre hangs out, and for some stupid reason you think you can just fuck with people's lives. Well I am sick and tired of people fucking with me and mine." He stood up bringing Simms up off the ground as if he were a toy.

"Now we are going to go outside and get into your Jeep. You are going to take us to this Tigre. You aren't going to warn him we are coming, and you aren't going to do a fucking thing that might get Eva hurt, do you understand me?"

Simm's eyes were as round as golf balls as he shook his head yes. Treb lowered him until his feet touched the ground. Then he eased his grip.

"Now stop playing fuckin' G-men and help us and we'll be out of your lives."

Simms looked at Rabbit with a question in his eyes.

"Jake," Rabbit said, "what the fuck, this man saved my ass a dozen times. Let's tell them what the fuck they want to know."

"Okay, okay," he said, " I had to be sure of who you guys were. This is pretty sensitive shit going on down here. You understand, don't you?"

Treb looked down at him. "Fuck the speech," he said, "let's just get moving."

They all started towards the door. About halfway across the room Simms reached under his shirt and before anyone realized it he had his pistol aimed at Treb.

"No one tells me what the fuck to do, asshole, now you.."

231

Before he could finish his sentence a blow came from behind him and stopped him cold. He dropped to the floor unconscious.

It was Rabbit.

"I'm sorry man," Rabbit said, looking at Dick, "he's just been down here too long. He doesn't realize what's real and what's a fucking game. Come on, I think I know where she is."

They looked at Simms laying lifeless on the floor. Rabbit dropped a twenty dollar bill on his chest and spoke to the girl behind the bar.

"Hey, Alma," he said, "put Jake to bed will you?"

On the way out the door he said, "She might as well, she's done it enough the past few months."

As the Jeep turned onto the highway Dick leaned forward from the backseat so he could hear what was being said in front.

"So you see," Rabbit was saying loudly so he could be heard over the engine and the wind," this Tirantia is a pretty bad dude. Number two in the Contras and trying for number one. When he got off the plane he had a girl with him. It had to be this girl you're looking for. Dark hair, striking blue/green eyes, nice body. That her?"

Treb just stared ahead. Dick said it was her.

"We don't know what he wanted her for, but he called her his 'secret weapon', whatever that means. You guys have any idea?"

Treb looked at Rabbit in the rearview mirror, "no, haven't a clue, do you?"

"No, but whatever he has planned, you can bet it's no good."

"Why did he blow up the boat in Emerald Bay?" Treb asked.

Rabbit sat quiet for a few seconds, feeling the big man's presence behind him more than ever. He slowed the Jeep down and pulled to the side of the

Emerald Bay

road, stopping. He stepped out of the Jeep and took out a cigarette. As he held a match to it he looked at the two men sitting in the Jeep.

He took a deep breath and started to talk.

"He ordered the boat blown up to kill the number one man, El Jeffe, and his two connections in the United States. The guys who would sell the cocaine and arrange for the weapons to be sent down here." He stopped for a second, thinking what he would say next, then he blurted it out.

"I set the charge on that boat," he said, and then he stood silently looking down.

Treb looked at him and then over at Dick. He looked confused. He'd been trying to find the men who had ruined his life and killed his wife and best friend, and now he had him in front of him.

Rabbit went on, almost babbling, "It was supposed to get them. We didn't know anyone else would be getting on the boat. We had orders from Kirkland at headquarters. Drug dealers, that was the target. Not innocent people. I don't want to kill innocent people...I . I ," he stopped and visibly calmed down, looking directly into Treb's eyes, "I'm sorry." It seemed so pitiful little to say, but it was all there was.

Treb sat back in the seat and looked at Rabbit. He wanted to feel hate. He wanted to feel anger. He felt almost guilty because he didn't. He felt sorry for the man.

"Rabbit," Treb said, "get in and let's go. We're wasting time."

As they drove Rabbit explained as much as he knew. "Tigre has set up a small camp just on this side of the Nicaragua border. It had five buildings and maybe 20 men there."

"Do you think that's where he'll have Eva?" Treb asked.

"Probably. What I can't figure out is why. Simms and I were working with him to rip off a shipment of cocaine. I guess you guys might as well know that. That's where the explosion came in. There was a fifty five gallon drum filled tight that sank right after the explosion. Only El Jeffe knows where it is and how to bring it up. I think somehow Tigre plans to use the girl to get this information out of Heffe, but neither Simms or I could figure out a connection."

"Well, whatever the deal is we get her back now. This CIA crap can wait," Treb said.

The rest of the trip was in silence. Each man's thoughts were his own.

After they pulled of the paved road they drove for a while on a dirt trail just wide enough for the Jeep to get through. Soon Rabbit pulled the Jeep off into a small clearing.

"Ok," he said, "It's right up there about a quarter of a mile. They have a guard that watches the road. From here we go on foot."

He walked to the back of the Jeep and pulled the spare tire forward on its swing out bracket. Then he reached under the rear bumper and pulled a lever. What looked like a section of the fuel tank pulled out like a drawer. He lifted the lid and there they saw a selection of weapons that would make Rambo shiver.

"Compliments of Uncle Sam," Rabbit said, and he selected a Mac 10 and four clips of ammo. "Help yourself, we're probably going to need it to get her out of there."

Treb reached in and took the other Mac 10 and a few clips of ammunition. Then he took a combat Colt .45 automatic and a Smith and Wesson .44 magnum. He liked the sound they made. Dick took a small cutoff Winchester pump action twelve gauge riot gun and filled a pouch with shells. Then he grabbed the LAWS Rocket launcher saying, "Well, you just never know, do you?"

They went through the brush and bushes to stay out of sight. Rabbit led them so they would pass where the lookout was posted and then came in on him from the rear.

"Tach two," he said to Dick, with a smile on his face.

Dick smiled back. Tach two was a plan they'd used back in 'Nam on outpost guards just like this one.

Rabbit walked around behind the guard and got in as close as he could, then Treb watched as Dick walked out onto the road right in front of the guard. At first the guard didn't see him, but when he did he looked as if he didn't believe his eyes. One minute he wasn't there, the next he was. The guard started to stand up as Rabbit hit him from behind. It was quiet and efficient.

They pulled the guard back into the underbrush and crept to where they could see the camp. There were four small huts and one larger than the rest. Parked in front of the largest was Tigre's Jeep.

"He's there," said Rabbit, "but we don't know if the girl's with him or not."

Treb smiled, "Well then, let's find out."

A man was walking from one of the huts to the edge of the jungle, probably to take a leak. Treb worked his way around to where the man was heading. As the man stood with his pecker in his hand watering the shrubs, Treb grabbed him form behind with one hand over the man's mouth, then jammed the barrel of his .44 Magnum into the man's scrotum from behind.

In Spanish Treb told him to remain still or have his balls blown up through his throat. The man nodded his head violently.

Treb took the gun and put it in the man's back, leading him back to where Dick and Rabbit waited.

"I think we have a friend here," he jammed the gun into the man's mouth, "yes; amigo?"

The man stared with eyes like saucers.

"Now my friend," Treb continued, "does Tigre have a girl in there with him?"

The man nodded his head that he did.

"And how many other are in there with him?" Treb asked in a friendly voice.

The man held up three fingers.

"One more question and we'll let you go. Why does he have this girl?"

The man looked at him for a minute, and then he shrugged his shoulders as if to say, "who knows."

"Thank you for your assistance," Treb said sarcastically, and he brought the butt of his gun down on the base of the man's skull.

The large hut had only one door, and it was facing the center of the compound. They looked around and studied the layout.

"Our only chance is to wait until dark. There are too many surprises in the daylight. By the time we got in she'd be dead." Treb checked his watch, "looks like an hour before sunset, and another thirty minutes until it's dark. We'd better tie up our friend or kill him."

Rabbit looked at the man laying on the ground.

"Let's ties him up, there's been enough killing."

As the darkness fell over the jungle the noises increased. Birds called and insects screamed, and a hundred small creatures moved from daylight into dark.

The three men moved around to the rear of one of the huts. A large fire was blazing in front of the large one, lighting up the whole camp. The men made their final plans and checked their watches.

Each man moved around the camp to where they were supposed to be. At the given time Dick raised the LAWS and aimed it at the nearest hut to the main cabin. He counted down, and right on schedule he saw Dick running across the open into the hut opposite the compound and Rabbit into the one next to it. He pulled the trigger and the shell launched itself heading straight for its target. At about the same time Treb and Rabbit entered their target huts, the third hut blew sky high.

Dick dropped the empty carcass of the gun and grabbed his riot gun, running across the open area unseen. All the people from the last hut, about six men, were coming out to see what happened at the other hut.

They didn't know what hit them as Dick pumped four rounds from the twelve gauge into the door area, and then plowed in with his pistol in hand.

Treb hit the door of his assigned hut and when he entered he saw three men playing cards. They looked up at the big man in sheer terror. The sound of his .44 Magnum filled the tent.

As Rabbit went into the final hut he found four people. Two men and two women. He held his gun on them and had them turn around. As they did so he knocked the two men over the head with the butt of his gun. He hesitated a minute, and then knocked out the two women. He felt better because at least he didn't kill them.

The three men came out of the huts at about the same time. The three guards from inside the hut were waiting by the door. They started firing. Treb, Dick, and Rabbit dropped behind the well and used it as a shield, returning fire.

All of a sudden Treb shouted, "Hey, the Jeep. It's Eva and Tigre!"

While the guards kept them pinned down behind the well, Tirantia and Eva had started the Jeep and were heading north on the dirt road.

Treb jumped up and charged the three men. He was almost demented. To be so close and then lose her.

He shot two of the men as he ran across the open area between them, and then, when he reached the doorway he grabbed the last man, gripping him by the neck and squeezing. Shaking the man like a rag doll.

"Where are they going? Where? Tell me or I'll break your fucking neck," he was screaming.

Dick put his hand on Treb's shoulder trying to calm him down.

"Hey, bro, calm down. You already did break his neck. The man's dead."

Treb looked at his friend and his eyes started to come back to normal.

He released the man and his body fell like a sack of potatoes.

Treb leaned against the wall and stared down the trail that the Jeep had gone down.

"By the time we'd get out Jeep we'd never find em," he said," Hey, Rabbit, what if we..."

Treb stopped in mid sentence.

Rabbit was laying face down about halfway between the doorway and the well..

Treb and Dick ran over to the man, rolling him over carefully. He had a bullet in his stomach. All three men knew it was fatal.

Rabbit's eyes opened and he looked up, trying to say something. He pulled Dick's ear down to his mouth and breathed something, then his breath let out and he was dead.

"What'd he say? Does he know where they went?"

Dick looked at Treb and shook his head slowly.

"No," Dick turned and started to walk to the Jeep,' he asked me to forgive him."

30

El Jeffe sat in his favorite chair and watched a gecko lizard stalking a large bug across the wall. He looked at his watch. It was 11:30. Tigre would be there in exactly a half hour.

There was the sound of a vehicle pulling up in front of his cabin and he heard people arriving. With Tigre's penchant for time he knew it wasn't him.

There was a knock at the door. He rose and put his hand on his sidearm as a matter of habit.

One of the guards came in.

"El Jeffe, there are three men to see you. Americans."

Heffe walked to the door and looked out into the

courtyard. There were three men standing by the jeep with his guards watching them with rifles. One was Simms, his contact with the US CIA. The other two he didn't recognize.

"Bring them in," he told the guard, "and keep two men in here to watch them."

The men were brought in and stood across the table from him as he sat in his chair.

"Well," he asked Simms, "have you found out what happened in Emerald Bay yet?"

"No," he said, "I'm sorry El Jeffe, but these men forced me to bring them here. They are looking for some silly girl that they say Tigre kidnapped in the United States." He shrugged his shoulders as if to say 'what could I do?' and then went on. "I know it is stupid, but they think you may have the girl."

"Girl? What are you talking about? I don't know of any gringa around here."

"We know Tigre had her," Treb said, "and he's your man. Where is she?"

"What is this girl to you," he asked the men standing in front of him. "Why did you come all the way down here and risk your life for a girl?"

They were silent.

El Jeffe looked at them. He didn't like Simms. He didn't trust him, but it was obvious these men didn't like him either, and Simms didn't care for them at all.

He looked at the biggest man. He was built stronger and bigger than any man he had ever seen. How does a man get like that? He asked himself. The other man had the look of a panther ready to spring. He was oriental looking but he looked as if he had Spanish blood also. Interesting, and his eyes were strong and hard. Also, El Jeffe thought, honest.

"What is it you want with this girl?" he asked them.

"Do you know where she is?" the big man asked.

"Perhaps, but I am the one asking questions here.

What do you want with this girl?" El Jeffe repeated.
"We came to take her home," the big man said.
"And where is home?"
"On a small island of the coast of California. Catalina," Treb answered.
El Jeffe looked shaken all of a sudden. Everyone in the room could see it.
"Catalina Island? This is your home? And the girl too?"
He sat back in his chair and looked at the men, not saying anything.
Treb tried to judge the distance from his hands to the guard's gun nearest him. It looked like he could get it without much trouble. All he could do was hope Dick realized what he was doing and could get the other one. All of a sudden the big man reached over to the nearest guard and snatched his rifle out of his hands in less than a second. Dick was just as fast, and had the second guard disarmed. Simms just stood there watching.
Treb held his gun on El Jeffe while Dick watched the guards.
"Simms," Treb said, "tie them up," indicating the guards.
"Now we will ask some questions," Treb said.
El Jeffe just looked at the big man with no fear at all.
"What is it you would like to know?" he asked.
"First of all, why would your second in command kidnap a girl in the US and bring her down here? What do you two want with her?"
El Jeffe looked at Treb for a minute, and then he answered.
"My friend, as to why Tigre kidnapped her, it is simple. He wanted to use her to make me tell him where $5,000,000 worth of cocaine is located off the island of Catalina, so he had a big reason, yes?"
"Why would his having Eva make you tell him

anything? What is she to you?"

El Jeffe looked in the big man's eyes.

"Eva? Eva is her name?" He smiled to himself. Eva had been his mother's name.

"She is my daughter."

Now all three men stood and stared at him. Simms more than the others.

"Your daughter?" Simms said, "where did you get a daughter? I know your file better than anyone, and you have no family. No children. How's this possible?"

"Mr. Simms, you are working with Tigre to take the cocaine for yourselves. I know this." Tigre looked at the man as if he were a pile of horse manure. "You have no honor," he continued. "I will talk with you no more."

"As for you two, I think you are sincere. I am more surprised than any of you to find this girl is my daughter, but it is so. Tigre has been trying to blackmail me into giving him the cocaine or he says he will kill her."

Treb and Dick both lowered their rifles. It was obvious the man was telling the truth.

El Jeffe went on, "They are due here in," he looked at his watch, "three minutes. Tigre is prompt if nothing else."

There was a knock at the door. A guard opened it a little and told him a Jeep was coming into the compound.

As Treb turned to look at the door Simms reached for his rifle trying to pull it from his hand. Treb tightened his grip and snatched it back out of the smaller man's grip. Then he slammed the butt down on Simm's head, knocking him to the ground, unconscious.

When Tigre walked into the cabin he was greeted by Treb and Dick standing near the door, holding their guns on him. He walked in and looked unconcerned.

"El Jeffe," he started to speak, "these men shot up my camp and killed many of my men. I see they have you prisoners also. Who are they?"

"Tigre, my friend, they do not have me prisoner. It is you they hold the guns on."

"Me, Heffe,? You know of course that this means your daughter will die? How can you allow this?"

"The choice is not mine. You see, the big man standing here before you is the girls' betrothed. He has come to get her. There is nothing I an do."

Tigre continued to play the game even though the odds were turning against him. He was prepared

"So," he turned to Treb, "she is your woman, yes?"

Treb just nodded his head.

Tigre's face turned ugly all of a sudden.

"Well, if you want to see her again, alive, I suggest you put down those guns and let us talk like civilized men," he waited a second and then shouted, "now, put them down or she dies." He held a remote detonation device in his hand.

"Did you think I was stupid to walk in here to be killed? This is my insurance. She is handcuffed to my Jeep and there is enough explosives to turn her into fumes, you understand?"

Treb and Dick slowly lowered their rifles.

"The pistols also," Tigre indicated.

They took them out and dropped them on the floor.

"Ok, now let us talk business," Tigre smiled, "I want the release device and the location of the cocaine. When I have these I will turn the girl over to you and you two can fight over her," he waited, holding a full house that he knew would take the pot.

"I am sorry my friend, that you have had to go through all this trouble, but I am afraid what you ask is not possible," El Jeffe said.

"Not possible? What are you talking about? You cut

the cocaine loose from the ship and you stashed the release device. You told me you did. Now you will turn them over to me or your daughter dies, in pieces. Don't you understand this."

"Yes, my friend, I understand, but I'm afraid you don't understand. I cannot give you what you want because it is not there. I don't have it."

"Where the hell is it?" Tigre screamed, losing his command.

"I have it," a deep voice rumbled from out of the next room.

Everyone in the cabin turned to look at the doorway, and Sheriff Bob Fox walked in smiling.

Fox walked over to El Jeffe who stood to embrace him. "Foxfire. It has been too long, yes?"

Treb and Dick just stood there with their mouths hanging open, staring.

Tigre pressed the detonator in his hand. Nothing happened. He looked very confused as Eva walked in through the door Fox had come through earlier. She walked over to Treb and gave him a long kiss holding him tight.

Then she walked to her new found father. "Senor, it is a great honor at last to meet you."

Fox looked at the confused faces on Treb and Dick.

"You thought I was just a bumbling small town sheriff? Thank you. I must have played the part well," he smiled a fatherly smile. "Actually, I was El Jeffe's US counterpart. That's the only reason we let the drugs come into the country so easy. They used 'my' island and after each drop I would inform the DEA where to find the goods. That way my friend here got his weapons, and we took hundreds of pounds of cocaine off the market."

, "Amigo," Heffe asked Fox," How is it you found my daughter? I didn't even know I had a daughter."

"An accident of fate. She was on the other boat in

the harbor when the boat blew up."

"And the boat," Heffe asked, "it was your thought? Tigre was attempting to kill me and take over, is this right?"

"I'm afraid so, my friend."

While they were talking Tigre Tirantia eased his way out the door. He ran to his Jeep and started the motor and swung the vehicle out of the compound.

"Hey!" Treb shouted when he noticed the man's absence. "Tigre's gone. He's the one I was looking for all the time!"

"Don't worry," said Fox, "You got him. You know when he flipped the detonator to blow Eva up in the Jeep?"

Treb just looked at him.

"Well," continued Fox, "I didn't disarm the bomb in the Jeep. I just put a five minute delay timer in the line."

Just then Jake Simms started to come to. He opened his eyes and saw Fox standing in front of him.

"Mr. Roberts," he said in a shocked voice, "you were going to buy the cocaine form me. It was you who double crossed us."

"Simms," smiled El Jeffe, "allow me to introduce my long time friend, Mr. Bob Fox. I believe you know him as 'Foxfire'?"

Just then the sound of Tigre's Jeep exploding filled the compound.

• Epilogue •

The pirate Hypolyte Blanchard had pulled into Emerald Bay to get away from the ships following him from Santa Cruz. He didn't know the troubles that lay before him or the fortunes he would leave for four people some 170 years later.

He only wanted some water and game to see he and his men south to San Diego harbor. He was almost the last of the breed and the last pirate to visit the Pacific Coast of California.

But the fates were not with Mr. Blanchard. Not at all.

When he anchored in Emerald Bay he sent a crew ashore to fill the water barrels. They had to hike up the cliffs and carry the barrels far inland, but it had to be done. As Captain, he ran his ship with an iron hand.

Some of his crew thought there was a little too much iron in those hands, so they decided to help themselves to the small treasure box they had taken off a trading ship bound for San Francisco from China. Less than 900 pieces of gold that would be shared by the ship's crew of 30 men when they reached San Diego. Not enough, some thought, and two of them stole into the captain's cabin late that night and liberated the small chest.

They lowered it over the side into a small boat and started to row ashore, but the fates weren't with the crew that trip. They were spotted by a lookout on the boat and in order to make time they dropped the chest over the side of the dinghy as they rowed ashore.

They were caught a day later and killed before they could tell their ex-shipmates where the gold had been dropped.

As the crew of the ship searched for the treasure a Santa Ana storm blew in from the north-north-east and it blew hard. The shallow anchorage became to dangerous to stay in, so the caption hoisted anchor and put to sea to save his ship and his crew.

As they were blown past Ship Rock they hit an edge of the then uncharted rock and tore a small hole in the bottom of the boat. With the wind blowing them out into the channel they fought to keep afloat, but to no avail. She sank in the San Pedro Channel with all hands, and over the next hundred years the current moved her steadily south, past her one time destination of San Diego, and into the rift between the Coronado Islands, where she has been lodged ever since.

The same storm caused such waves as to push the box filled with gold across Indian Reef, until it dropped of the side of the reef and fell, becoming lodged in a crevice about seventy five feet down, and there it was was covered with sand from the large waves washing on beach.

For sixty three years the box buried there, for any who would swim by to find under just a few feet of sand. But it went undiscovered. Then the biggest earthquake in over two hundred years shook the coast in 1881, pushing the Channel Islands a full three feet closer to Alaska. The Pacific Plate gave and shook until those who lived there thought it was the end of the world.

And the little chest full of gold was closed up in a dark jumble of rocks where it laid, buried for the next hundred years. The explosion that killed Karen loosened those rocks, and as they fell they crushed the now rotten chest, spilling the gold to the ocean's floor.

.....

Two good friends were diving one day, off the reef at Emerald Bay. They had just returned from a little trip to Central America.

Sheriff Fox, retired CIA, sat and talked with the two prettiest girls on the beach about a pair of childhood sweethearts who found each other in San Salvadore after 20 years of separation. Meanwhile, two friends went down to see if they could find how a single gold coin had come to be found after having lain there, undiscovered, for over 170 years.

-End-